Jeremy Camp LLC
2021 21st Avenue South, Suite 311
Nashville Tennessee 37212

ISBN (10-digit) 0615468667
ISBN (13-digit) 9780615468662
Paperback

Jeremy Camp, with Phil Newman

Printed in the United States of America

First printing 2011

Book design by Birdsong Creative, Inc.
Franklin, TN | www.birdsongcreative.com

Photographs of author by Laura Dart

D0188041

Table of Contents

foreword

I remember where I was when the walls came crashing in. Sitting in my office staring at my computer and a file of payroll documents realizing that the impossible had happened. I had been embezzled out of more than $40,000. It wasn't the loss of funds that caused the blood to drain from my face that afternoon. Rather it was the fact that the loss had come at the hands of someone I had trusted.

In my life I can count on one hand the times when I felt my world tilt hard off its axis, when breathing required my concentration and all logic and order spun crazily out of control. This was one of those times.

Back then, I didn't know Jeremy Camp as a friend the way I do now. But I knew him as a musician, the depth of his music and the hope in his story. I was aware of his very great loss in watching his young wife die of cancer, and I was moved by his determined effort to praise God anyway.

For that reason, as I stared into the screen disbelieving what I was seeing and trying to slow my racing heart, a single thought came to mind: I needed to hear Jeremy's music. I needed it like I needed to breathe. Without waiting a moment longer I went to my computer where my iTunes library is stored, and I burned a CD with just three songs—all by Jeremy: "Walk by Faith," "Give Me Jesus" and "I Still Believe." As the CD popped out of my computer, I grabbed a Sharpie and wrote just one word across the silver disc:

Help.

See, many times that's how the Holy Spirit works among us, by reminding us that someone else survived a loss in the power of God. And so, we can be certain that He will help us do the same.

That night we had tickets to a basketball game. I was so devastated by the revelation of this theft in my life that I didn't tell the kids. I couldn't. My brain barely allowed the reality to work its way into my conscious. I told just the bare details to my husband, assuring him I would go into depth later. The truth was, I couldn't bear to go into detail then. Not while my world was still collapsing around me.

Instead of talking about it or examining it or trying to imagine how something like that could have happened, I played my *Help* CD loud and long, over and over and over again. *I will walk by faith...even when I cannot see...and I still believe in Your faithfulness...I still believe in Your truth...I still believe in Your Holy Word...even when I cannot see...I still believe.*

Over and over and over again.

By the end of the night I was OK. My world was right-side up again and I could factually grasp the idea that a trusted person had stolen...not from me, but from God. That person would have the Lord to deal with, and God would protect me, my family, and my ministry. With God on our side, we would get through this—the same as any of us can get through anything that comes our way as long as we still believe.

I will never forget how Jeremy's story, his music and his testimony helped me through that time in my life. We have choices when life hits us with a tsunami of tragedy or despair, crisis or loss. That's the message of Jeremy Camp's book, and it's the reason you will find hope and healing by journeying through the pages of his story, his personal tsunami.

Take this book slowly. Savor the real story and the way God carried Jeremy through it. And as you do, remember to sing these words in the darkest of nights:

Even when I cannot see...I still believe.

—Karen Kingsbury

New York Times *bestselling author Karen Kingsbury is America's Favorite Inspirational Novelist and author of* Unlocked *and* Shades of Blue, *along with the Baxter Family series. She has written more than 50 of her Life-Changing Fiction™ titles, and there are nearly 15 million copies of her books in print. Learn more about Karen at KarenKingsbury.com or on Facebook.*

PROLOGUE

It's Time

I'm not exactly sure how many minutes had passed when one of the friends gathered next door peeked into the room where I lay sprawled on the floor, crying out to God, weeping and longing.

"Jeremy," my friend said softly, "it's time."

I rose and walked back toward the other room, crying all the way. I couldn't believe it, but I knew: The moment had arrived to say goodbye to my wife.

PART 1

CHAPTER 1

Hoosier Sweet Home

*T*he journey that led me to that moment of desperation in a Southern California hospital room had begun 23 years earlier in the small, Midwestern town of Lafayette, Indiana.

I was born there on January 12, 1978, into an amazing Christian family. For as long as I can remember, my dad, Tom, was always involved in ministry, and my mom, Teri, seemed to have a direct line to God through her hours of prayer and time spent soaking in the Scriptures. The most important aspect of life in our home was Jesus. Today, my dad is the pastor of Harvest Chapel in Lafayette, a local fellowship that he started in 1993.

What's really mind-blowing is how *completely* messed up my parents' lives were up until a year before I was born. I hope sharing some of their story here—the dark, destructive path they were walking and the hope they discovered that changed everything—will illustrate the incredible miracle that God worked in their lives, in our family, and ultimately in my own life.

Collision Course

Each of my parents had grown up without knowing the Lord. As a teenager, my dad was heavily into alcohol and drugs, and he dropped out of school. He was a burly, long-haired, likeable guy whose friends called him "Bear." The only time he wasn't so likeable was when he had been drinking hard liquor, which he did now and then.

My mom led a much different early life, on the "opposite side of the tracks" from my dad. She was a more straight-laced girl who came from a stable home and had goals for the future. A good student in school, she had been accepted to Purdue University before beginning to date my dad when she was a senior in high school. She was drawn to him because he was so easy to talk to. When they became a couple, lots of people around them wondered why such a "good girl" as Teri would go out with such a "rebel" as Bear Camp.

They had reason to worry. My dad wasn't a great influence on my mom. He not only drank and smoked pot; he also did other drugs and gradually got into dealing them. The couple moved in together, and their place became Party Central. My mom worked low-paying jobs (long-distance operator, hospital assistant) while my dad picked up sporadic construction work—nothing steady, though, since he was high much of the time.

In 1975, after my sister April was born, the partying at home slowed down a little bit, but my dad was still headed for trouble. By the fall of 1976, he was drinking more heavily than ever, doing cocaine, selling it, and becoming violent. On two occasions, he tore up a hotel room.

One day he came home and sunk down into a chair. "I don't know what's wrong with me," he said to my mom. "I feel so empty inside. It's not you. It's not April. These drugs are doing it. I'm not a good father to my daughter. I'm not married. I've made a mess of everything."

When Christmas Day 1976 arrived, he was so depressed that my mom thought he might try to harm himself. But he surprised her by saying, "I have to go to a church. I need to talk to a minister."

Those words shocked her. Church hadn't really occurred to her, but she was open to anything that might help.

After visiting two churches that weren't really the right fit for two hippies, my mom mentioned to my dad, "Some people at my job have been telling me about Jesus and their church, and they said we could come as we are, no matter what we look like or dress like. Could we try it out?" He agreed.

Rescued

It was January 2, the first Sunday of 1977. That morning, my dad had gone to help a buddy move. He stayed out all afternoon. When it was about time to go to church that evening, he called my mom at home.

"Hey, I'm at a Mexican restaurant," he said, slurring his words.

"Have you been drinking?" she asked.

"Oh, just a little," he said. "Don't worry, I'll pick you up and we'll all go." Now he sounded *really* intoxicated.

My mom was angry, and she started crying. "There's no *way* I'm going to church with you guys!" she said, and hung up. She left to go to church alone.

About 300 people were gathered for worship and teaching that night. My mom sat toward the back, in the middle of a row. A few minutes into the service, she heard a commotion and glanced over her shoulder. It was my dad and his buddy, as drunk as could be, stumbling in. She slid down, but they saw her and started climbing over the pews to get to her. When they arrived and plopped down, my dad's inebriated friend started talking loudly. An usher walked up the aisle and asked him to come sit next to him, which he did. My mom was reeling. It felt like a circus.

About that time, the pastor began to preach. His message was about being delivered from the bondage of drugs and alcohol. Seriously! A few sentences in, my mom looked beside her and noticed that my dad had begun to sob. Throughout the message, he cried and cried and cried, burying his head in his hands.

When the "altar call" arrived at the end of the message, a youth pastor came up to them and asked, "Do you want to go forward?" My dad didn't need any coaxing. He jumped up and literally *ran* down the aisle to the front. His buddy wasn't far behind. My mom walked after them. The whole church came down and began to pray for them as my dad and his friend received the gift of new life in Jesus.

After the service, church leaders encouraged them with words of kindness and wisdom. They gave them a copy of *The Living Bible* and told them to start with the Gospel of John.

In this Assemblies of God church, the pastor had been praying for revival. That night, it descended on the church. The pastor couldn't stand alcohol, and he wasn't crazy about long-haired hippies. So, whom did the Lord use to bring revival? Who else: *Drunk hippies*. From that season, the church would launch a "Whosoever Ministry"—based on the idea that whosoever God brings into your path, *that's* who you reach out to with the love of Jesus.

Absorbing the news of my dad's conversion that night, my mom reacted with a kind of detached approval. Her attitude was, "Those guys *sure* needed that." But over the next week, as she read the Gospel of John—once she started, she couldn't put it down—her eyes were open to the fact that *she* was a sinner in need of a perfect Savior, too. When she realized what Christ had done for her, it hit her hard.

One night, she sat in her living-room chair and cried out, "Lord, I am so sorry!" That was the clincher for her. At that moment she surrendered completely and prayed, "I will go anywhere, do anything. Whatever You ask, I'm Yours."

Those few weeks marked a drastic change in my parents' lives. Three weeks later, on January 22, 1977, they exchanged vows and were married in that church. A year and ten days after they got saved, I was born. By then, they were well on their way to laying the foundation for our family with Christ at the center.

I am so glad I came along *after* God got hold of my parents. I only know about their pre-salvation struggles through stories and photos. What I remember most is being raised in a home where my mom and dad were on fire with the love of Jesus and a desire to share it with others. My dad always seemed to have a shepherd's heart, even though he wasn't a pastor yet when I was a child. My parents weren't perfect, of course, but I knew where their hearts and minds were focused. They put the Lord first. What I saw when we went to church together was exactly what I saw at home. They were genuine, sold-out followers of Jesus.

Fed By Faith

I am the second of four children. In addition to my older sister, April, I have two younger brothers, Jared and Joshua.

Josh has Down syndrome, and he is an incredible blessing to me and to our whole family. We all share tons of happy memories from childhood, even though it wasn't an easy or comfortable life. My family was *super poor*. My dad was barely literate, and he didn't have a formal education or any particular technical skills—he miraculously passed his general equivalency diploma (GED) test well into adulthood—so he bounced from odd job to odd job, doing whatever work he could land. His income was sparse and infrequent.

This isn't one of those sob stories that I want you to hear and go, "Awwwwwww." While we didn't have a lot of material comforts, the truth is that being poor gave us the opportunity to see God move in many ways that we might not have experienced otherwise. We truly lived by faith, because we had no other choice.

There were times when we wouldn't have money for food from Tuesday until payday on Friday. The cupboards would be bare, and that's no exaggeration. Without saying anything to anyone outside of our family, my parents would initiate a time of prayer. We would get on our knees and pray that God would provide food for us. Sometimes—fairly often, it seemed like—we would wake up the next morning and find that people had set groceries on our front porch.

People gave us other stuff, too...including many interesting vehicles. We had about fifteen different cars when I was a kid—cars like rusty Ford Pintos and barely running Chevys. They would last about a year before dying, but we were thankful for each one of them.

Our auto adventures gave us lots of opportunities to create lasting memories. For example, one day my mom drove our hand-me-down Pinto to pick up my sister and two of her friends from Girls Scouts. After the girls climbed into the car, my mom noticed that one of April's second-grade friends was looking around the back seat with big eyes.

"Um, where did you get this car?" the little girl asked.

"Oh, a friend gave it to us," my mom replied.

The girl looked around the car again and, in a cute little voice just loud enough to be heard, said, "Hmmm, some friend." My mom smiled and chuckled up in the front seat.

Another day, my mom picked me up from church in a different clunker. The floorboards were so rusted out that I could see the ground under my feet. No joke. As I got in and closed the passenger-side door, I noticed a belt hanging from the door.

"What's this?" I asked.

She said, "You gotta hold on to it. Buckle up and hang on to the belt, because if you don't, the door will fly open when we go around curves." I held on to that piece of fake leather like my life depended on it. It probably did.

Okay, here's the last car story, but it has *got* to be the harshest one for a teenage boy to deal with: One day when I was in seventh grade, I was hanging out after school talking with my girlfriend at the time. She was a cheerleader, and I was this ultra-cool, stud football player. (We had the kind of relationship where you are "going out" but not really going anywhere.) All of a sudden here comes my dad to pick me up, driving a Pinto that sounded about as loud as a drag racer. The muffler had fallen off some time before. All of the kids hanging around turned to look at the rusty, beat-up car as I walked over and tried to open the passenger-side door as quickly as I could. It wouldn't open (surprise), so I had to climb into the car through the window. This was not exactly a popularity boost for a 13-year-old boy.

Sometimes I felt embarrassed about being poor, but looking back now I can laugh and give thanks that we had *any* cars to get us around and *any* food to eat. Tough situations like those can build our character and prepare us for harder days to come. Not only that, but the kind of faith my parents showed me in our home was *real*, and it stuck with me. Just like a lot of kids, I went through a "punk stage" when I was ungrateful and bummed about all the things my family couldn't afford. But now, I am so incredibly thankful for those lean times. Little did I know that having nothing else except for God to lean on was providing much-needed preparation for what I would walk through later in life.

A Sure Foundation

My parents also instilled the word of God into my life early on. Having come out of such a messed-up background and then getting radically saved, they knew the impact of putting down deep roots in the Scriptures. They hosted a Friday-night Bible study just about every week (to replace the wild parties they had hosted on Fridays before coming to know Christ). People would hang out until three or four in the morning—talking about God, singing, praying.

I gave my heart to the Lord when I was four or five years old, knowing what I was doing. What it meant to say "yes" to Jesus had been explained to me, and I was as receptive and knowledgeable as any young child could be. I can't even remember what it felt like *not* to have faith and trust in the Lord as my foundation.

When I entered adolescence, a few bombs came flying into the mix trying to blow up that solid foundation. In junior high school, I started to stray. I had always been a "church kid," but

I went wayward for a period of about three years. To be honest, I just really wanted to explore what the world had to offer. I got involved in school sports, especially football. Football and all that goes with it—the coolness, the swagger, the popularity—became a big part of my identity. I wanted to be liked, to run with the "in" crowd. I also started partying pretty hard.

Don't get me wrong: It's not as if I forgot about God. I always had the knowledge that I was out on a shaky limb during this rebellious season. I experienced times of repentance when I would cry out, "God, I'm tired of this junk! I'm sorry. I don't want to do this anymore."

But then I would go right back to school and get sucked back into what I had been doing. My parents didn't know everything. I tried to keep my wandering a secret, because I didn't want to let them down. (Later on, they told me they'd been aware that I was veering into dangerous territory as my teen years progressed. The Lord revealed to their hearts that all was not right, and they asked Him for wisdom about how much space to give me.)

Up to that point, I had done everything pretty well. I was a "good kid." I didn't want to get caught, either. I knew my family was the real deal, on the right path, with solid answers about life. *I was the one acting like an idiot*, playing the role of prodigal in search of the next thrill.

Whenever God would press on me with conviction, I would confess my sin and return to Him...but then I would slip right back out of His arms. I wanted to do right, but I couldn't. Paul's words were true of me:

"When I want to do good, evil is right there with me.
For in my inner being I delight in God's law; but I see

another law at work in the members of my body, wag-
ing war against the law of my mind and making me a
prisoner of the law of sin at work within my members.
What a wretched man I am! Who will rescue me from
this body of death? Thanks be to God—through Jesus
Christ our Lord!"[1]

Wretched is exactly how I felt most of the time through ninth and tenth grades—never really happy for more than a few fleeting moments. The fun never seemed to last. I was aware of what I was doing. I knew it didn't line up with who God wanted me to be, but I wasn't angry at Him. I realized my own curiosity had led me to a search for meaning outside the safe bounds of His ways. James expresses it well in his New Testament book: "...each one is tempted when, by his own evil desire, he is dragged away and enticed."[2]

I needed a lifeline, and—just in time—one was about to be tossed my way.

[1] *Romans 7:21-25*
[2] *James 1:14*

CHAPTER 2

Take Me Back?

M y uneasiness during this time came to a head in the summer of 1994. I had finished my sophomore year at our public high school, feeling like a fairly cool 16-year old, when I was invited to travel to a Christian youth camp in California. Of course my first thought wasn't, "Wow, a chance to pray and worship with a bunch of on-fire believers and get right with God." It was more like: "Cali? Cool place to hang. I'm there!"

On my first night after arriving at the camp, as I watched all the kids around me lifting their hands and wor shipping Jesus, something started to stir within me. I knew my heart was full of crud that was far removed from such tender devotion. Shame began to well up in my soul. I didn't just feel convicted, though. I also felt drawn toward the love and grace and truth that the other kids were celebrating in God's presence.

Later, as I listened to the speaker talk about "giving all of ourselves to God," I knew something totally radical was unfolding. The Lord began speaking to my heart, gently but firmly: "Jeremy, I want to use you, but you are teetering on the edge. You need to *run*. Run away from the lure of the world, and run back to Me. I'm right here, waiting for you."

That night, I said "yes" to Him again. Yes, I would come back to what I knew was right. Yes, I would seek to walk by faith rather than pursuing popularity and coolness. Yes, I would follow the narrow way rather than dabbling in the world's alluring but unsatisfying pleasures.

I was so excited, and felt so free for the first time in several years, that I called my parents right away and told them what had happened. "My eyes are open, and I want to serve Him," I told them.

The rest of that week represented a 180-degree change. As it turned out, it *was* great to be around a bunch of kids who loved Jesus, worshipping God and getting right with Him. The speaker, Jon Courson, taught from the book of Revelation, zooming in on the church's waywardness and the need for followers of God to be purified. I lost count of the number of times I thought, *Oh my gosh, that's me. Are you talking directly to ME?*

The Scriptures we studied that week included a reference to the church at Laodicea, whose spiritual vitality was as unappealing as lukewarm food. The Lord responded to that fake, shallow devotion by saying, "I will vomit you out of my mouth."[3] Yeah, that sounds harsh, doesn't it? I had been like that church: neither hot nor cold, and therefore of little use to God. It felt like a warning in my heart. It wasn't that God was withholding His love from me—on the contrary, I was

---

[3] Rev. 3:16

         I STILL BELIEVE

beginning to realize how deeply He loved me—but I felt that He was warning me. *What am I doing?* I thought. *All of these things are SO empty. It's time for a new start and a whole new way of living.*

I Know the Plans...

For the rest of the summer of '94, seeds of faith began to sprout in my rededicated heart. But as the start of my junior year drew closer, I became seriously scared about the idea of going back to the same school where I had worked so hard to create a "cool, popular, partier" persona. I had a true desire to grow spiritually that school year, but I knew I could easily become distracted and drawn back into my former ways. The illustration that Jesus gave about sowing seeds played in my mind. I did not want to become like the seed planted among thorns that would be "choked with cares, riches, and pleasures of life, and bring no fruit to maturity."[4]

There was a Christian school near where we lived, and I told my parents I wanted to go there instead. They were sympathetic but told me we just couldn't afford the cost.

"Trust me," I told them, pleading, "I *can't* go to my old high school this year."

There seemed to be no other option, however, and so, on the first day of public school (the Christian school would start two weeks later), I reluctantly got dressed and waited for the bus. With each second, my fear about walking away from God again hit me like a wave.

"Mom, Dad, I can't do it," I blurted out. "I can't get on the bus!"

---

[4] *Luke 8:14*

My dad took a deep breath. "Okay," he said. "Let's pray and see if the Lord will open another way for us."

I was so thankful, but I had no idea where the money for private-school tuition, fees and books would come from. Based on what you've read so far, it won't surprise you to hear that the Lord provided. From several sources, the money I needed for books and fees came in.

I called the Christian school and asked if I could work to pay off my tuition—doing janitorial services or anything else that was needed. They agreed, and my parents enrolled me that day. I *knew* I was supposed to go to that school. I believed deep down that it was part of God's plan for me at that season of my life. A change of scenery was critical. Even though it took cleaning toilets and vacuuming floors to make it happen, it was well worth it.

God used that whole situation to deepen within me a strong sense of Jeremiah 29:11. "'For I know the plans I have for you,' declares the Lord, 'plans to prosper you and not to harm you, plans to give you hope and a future.'" He wants to use each of us in ways that bless *us* and bless *others*. He longs to give us the incredible satisfaction of being part of bringing Him glory and seeing His kingdom advanced. I started to understand that, in bits and pieces.

Notes, Chords & Simple Songs

Because I was taking a year off from sports during eleventh grade (the private school didn't have football), my schedule was freed up for other pursuits. As a result, music became a more prominent part of my life. The seeds had been planted just a few years earlier. As I mentioned before, my main interests as a kid revolved around sports. Really, sports were my *life*. I didn't think too much about music until later. But ever since I was little, I had seen a guitar lying around the house. My dad played guitar, and he often led worship at church.

One day, when I was 14, I casually asked him, "Dad, do you think you could teach me some chords?" He agreed, and we sat down for our first informal lesson. I remember *really* enjoying it. After strumming my very first chord I told him, "This is awesome!"

Almost right away, I began to learn a few simple songs, mostly mainstream hits by artists like Pearl Jam, Aerosmith and Creedence Clearwater Revival (CCR), and other stuff I heard on the radio. We didn't have "secular" CDs at home. We listened almost exclusively to Christian-music artists like Mylon (LeFevre) & Broken Heart, DeGarmo & Key, Resurrection Band (also known as REZ Band), and others.

I always had more of a rock edge to what I liked to listen to and play. I had gone with my parents to the big Christian-music festivals Icthus (in Kentucky) and Cornerstone (in Illinois) since I was a kid, and had been exposed to a broad spectrum of Christ-centered rock music. In fact, I remember standing at Cornerstone one night and thinking, *"Someday, it would be cool to sing on that stage."* The Lord, in His goodness, would later make that childhood dream come true.

I also remember writing my first song, during one of those tough teenage times when I felt caught between walking with God and falling prey to the snares of the world. I called it "Set Me Free," and the simple lyric included these words:

> *I know your doors are open anytime I want to come in.*
> *But whenever I come close to you I turn back to sin.*
> *You've got to set me free...*

That basically sums up my adolescent cry. I wanted freedom. I had the desire to overcome distractions, to get off the fencepost, to stop serving two masters and follow the Lord wholeheartedly. That's the place where He finally took me, beginning with that summer camp in California.

One thing I realized when I wrote that first song was how natural it felt to write down how I was feeling. That approach laid the foundation of how I still write songs: with honest, emotional, gut-level lyrics about what God is doing and speaking into my life today.

Around the time of my junior year, I started a little garage band. For the life of me, I can't remember the name of that first group, but I do recall the name of my second band: Temple Rising. (Need I say more?) We played a lot of cover songs—but we didn't play them very well, at least not at first.

It wasn't long before I started writing songs anchored in Jesus and in my growing faith in Him. God was slowly shifting my primary passion into a desire for music. It became a way that I expressed what was going on in my heart.

My junior year at the private Christian school was a time of steady spiritual growth and musical exploration. Life seemed to be firing on all cylinders. Senior year, beginning the fall of 1995, was a little bit different story. I ended up going back to the public high school. Although I was stronger than before and committed to walking out my faith, it was still a challenging year. I struggled to stand firm in the face of "all that is in the world—the lust of the flesh, the lust of the eyes, and the pride of life."[5] I was so eager to get out of that school that I studied hard enough to graduate halfway through the year.

Future Dreams

During the early part of 1996, I found myself standing between two paths. One path would lead to Purdue University, maybe even trying out for the football team as a "walk on." The other would lead to Bible college to study the Scriptures. As I considered both possibilities and received guidance and input from my parents, Bible college became the leading option.

A pivotal point in this process was a dream I had one night. Even with my faith emerging, I was still struggling. I wasn't partying like I had two years before, but my thoughts and desires were conflicted. The battle raged within. I knew God had spoken to my heart at 16 when I had come back to Him in California. I remembered the good plans He had for me, but the enemy was trying to devour me and prevent God's plans from coming true.

In the dream, I was in the house with my mom, who was on the phone. She finished the call and hung up. I asked, "Who was that?" She looked at me and said, "It was Satan. Do you have his number?" I woke up in a cold sweat.

I wasn't sure what the dream meant—although it alarmed me—until about two weeks later, when God spoke

---

[5] 1 John 2:16

to my heart and basically interpreted it. The Lord doesn't often speak to me through dreams, by the way, but this time there was no mistaking His voice in my heart. He said, "You still have Satan's number. You haven't cut him off completely. It's time to move on, and *never...look...back.* I have a plan for you, and I want you to dig into My Word."

After that, it was crystal clear that I would go to Bible college. I wanted *all* of God, and I knew it would begin with knowing His truth. Thanks to my parents, I had grown up understanding the power of the Scriptures. I knew that the man who delighted in God's truth would bear fruit,[6] that His word would not return void but would accomplish much,[7] and that the Scriptures were sharper than any double-edged sword.[8] All those things coalesced, and I caught a vision for digging into the Bible to the fullest extent possible.

---

[6] *Psalm 1*
[7] *Isaiah 55*
[8] *Hebrews 4*

CHAPTER 3

Westward

I arrived at Calvary Chapel Bible College in Murrieta, California, in the fall of 1996, excited that God was calling me into ministry with such a solid foundation. Two years (four semesters) of Bible college awaited me. I wasn't thinking much about music then. I simply wanted to get out of the world, dig into the Word, and set the course for whatever lay ahead.

The time had come to separate myself and become purified. The psalms speak of a generation with clean hands and pure hearts — of people who don't lift our souls to idols, but who instead seek His face and make a lasting impact on our world.[9] *That's* who I wanted to be.

After being at Calvary for about a month, I felt that God really took me to a whole new level of freedom. All of those battles, all of the wandering, all of the fence-riding were behind me. I remember weeping for literally two hours straight

---

[9] *Psalm 24:4*

after one of my classes—not out of sadness, but out of repentance and cleansing. I still had junk in my life that God was purging. I finally had let Him really dig in deep and start to purify my heart.

From that point forward, man, it was *on*. I experienced amazing times of worship and fellowship, and a radical joy and confidence that I had not known before. I felt like Ezekiel, to whom God had made a promise: "I will give you a new heart and put a new spirit within you; I will take the heart of stone out of your flesh and give you a heart of flesh." [10] The words of Isaiah also echoed in my mind during this season: "Here am I. Send me!" [11] *Whatever you want, Lord, I'll do it. Wherever you want me to go, I'll go there.*

The classes I took taught the Bible, verse by verse and book by book, from Genesis to Revelation. We listened to Calvary Chapel leader Chuck Smith's teaching tapes and worked through the Scriptures.

Humbling Gifts

Keith March, a local doctor back home in Indiana, had generously agreed to pay for my first semester at college. After that, I was on my own. I got a job at Staples, stocking office supplies. Before my second year at Calvary, during the summer of 1997, I worked construction to pay for a third semester. After that, I worked out a deal to pay back my fourth semester after college so I could focus on my studies.

While I was at college, I didn't own a guitar. I would borrow one from friends when I led worship at school (about

---

[10] *Ezekiel 36:26*
[11] *Isaiah 6:8*

I STILL BELIEVE

twice a week) and to play out at churches, just as I had borrowed my dad's to play back in Lafayette. I simply couldn't afford my own yet. Honestly, it was tough enough just scraping together enough money to buy food.

Halfway through my second year of Bible college, I went home for the holidays. On Christmas morning, I was shocked to discover that my parents had bought me a new guitar—not just *any* guitar, but my *dream* guitar, a beautiful Taylor. I found out later that they had felt led to borrow money to buy it. It was a little over $2,000. They had no extra money at all, but they recognized what God was doing in my life through music and believed that the instrument would be a worthwhile investment in my future.

As the tears flowed in the family room and I shook my head in amazement, my heart almost burst with anticipation. *Lord, whatever You want. Not my plans, but Yours. Here I am. I can't wait to see what happens from here!*

As 1998 began, I was playing worship at church in Lafayette and getting together with a little band to jam. Doors were cracking open for music, and I was enjoying the feeling of playing more and more. I still had *no* clue that I might end up as a full-time musician; I was just having a blast.

I went back to California and finished the end of my second year at college that spring. During the summer and fall, I worked as a bagger at Vons Grocery Store, trying to pay off my school debt. I also got involved in the College and Career ministry at Calvary Chapel Vista. I would hang out, play music, help to lead worship, and jam with the guys.

One day in late autumn, singer/songwriter Jean-Luc Lajoie of The Kry came into Vista looking for musicians to play in a youth band. Someone—I'm not sure who—told him to "come back sometime and check out Jeremy Camp." He showed up one night while we were practicing. After we had finished he said, in his thick French accent, "That's a pretty good song."

Jean-Luc and I hit it off right away, not just musically but spiritually as well. I felt a sense of fellowship with him and thought, *Here's a cool bro who loves Jesus.* We became fast friends, and he invited me to play in the youth band that he was putting together.

You might think I would have jumped at the chance to play and sing in a band, especially one that was set up by a known artist like Jean-Luc. But I knew I needed to pray about it. I promised him that I would prayerfully consider the opportunity. But there were other possibilities as well. My dad had started Harvest Chapel five years earlier, and one option was to move back to Lafayette and work with him there. He encouraged me to seek the Lord about it, even as he admitted that his heart would love for Indiana to be God's answer.

In December of 1998, having quit my job at Vons and moved out of the place I had been staying, I flew home to Indiana, not knowing whether I would be coming back to the West Coast. My dad, my mom and I talked about the future around the kitchen table. As usual, my mom shared scripture after scripture that the Lord had given her. My dad, sensing this pivotal crossroads in his son's life, invited me to go with him to a friend's cabin for several days of fasting and prayer.

While I was at the cabin, God spoke clearly to my heart: "Go back to California." I questioned Him, struggling to be sure I was hearing correctly. *Are you sure, Lord? I moved out of my place. I am ready to serve here at Harvest. Do you really want*

a jobless, homeless dude heading back to California? As I got
quiet and listened for His voice, I began to feel a strong assurance that He had a plan for me and would provide exactly
what was necessary to accomplish it. My parents both agreed
with this direction and prayed over me as I made plans to go
West again.

Marge in Charge

I landed at the Ontario (California) Airport with one bag,
no home, and a thin itinerary—so thin, in fact, that it contained just one item: heading directly to a youth pastors' conference at the Bible college in Murrieta. Bryan, a friend from
California, picked me up at the airport and drove me to Calvary.

Walking around the conference, I bumped into another
friend, Isaiah Thompson, whom I had met at CC Vista. As if
on cue, he said, "Hey man, I heard that you need a place to
stay. My Grandma Marge needs someone to look after her—
buy groceries, take her to the doctor, that kind of stuff—and
she'll give you room and board. You up for that?"

"Wow, really?" I shrugged, mulling over my severely
limited options. "Okay, why not."

The next day, my youth pastor Dave Hole drove me to
the address Isaiah had given me. "I guess this must be the
place," I said as we pulled up to the house.

"Wait...you mean you've never been here before?" Dave
asked. "You don't know this lady at all?"

"Nope," I said, "but I guess this is where I'm gonna stay."

A smiling, gray-haired woman answered my knock on
the door.

"Hi, Marge? I'm Jeremy. I guess I'm going to be living
with you," I said.

"Oh," she said, "you have such beautiful eyes. Come on in."

We sat in her breakfast nook talking for an hour or so. She asked about me, so I told her about growing up in Indiana, coming out to California for Bible college, and playing music. She told me about her late husband, who had served in the military, and about her faith in the Lord.

"Let me show you to your room. If you want to go shopping for groceries tomorrow, here's my credit card."

Sitting quietly in my room, I took a deep breath. *All right, Lord, here I am. What do You have in mind?* I was about as close to broke as a guy could get; my bank account at the time was pushing $20. I had a cell phone—the only thing I owned—but no car. Boy, was I thankful for the live-in job with Marge!

An Open Door

I called Jean-Luc to tell him I was in town. As it turned out, the youth band he had been forming didn't come together, but Jean-Luc and I remained friends and began to spend time hanging out. One day he called with an offer.

"Hey, we're going to go do a concert," he said. "Would you like to come and help sell merch?"

My two-part answer—"Let me pray about it" and "Yes!"—came out pretty close to the same time. It went well, and one concert turned into more evenings with The Kry. Jean-Luc and his brother, Yves, paid me a little bit of money to help them out. Much more important than that, they poured into my life, spiritually and musically. I learned to play and sing better, and I saw how they lived out their faith with integrity both on and off the stage.

One afternoon before a concert, Jean-Luc said, "Hey, why don't you play a song tonight?"

I was a little bit stunned, but without hesitation I smiled and said, "I would *love* to."

It only happened a few times, but opening for The Kry boosted my confidence in playing to large audiences, and it led to my learning some of the band's songs and playing guitar along with their set, too. Even more amazing: If The Kry couldn't accept an invitation because of a scheduling conflict, Jean-Luc would often refer me.

One day, an acquaintance who had heard I needed a car called and offered to give me one to use. (I had been hitching rides or borrowing cars when I could.) I smiled as I remembered my family's revolving-vehicle adventures in Indiana. As my dad might put it, one of the songs I wrote later on that became well known could just as easily have been called "Drive By Faith."

Finally, I reached a point where I was playing enough music to survive—meaning I could pay for food, clothes and gas a week or two at a time. God was opening doors. We had a great group of guys in our College and Career group at Vista, and our times of praise to the Lord were awesome. Things were good. I loved going with the flow, stepping out in faith, playing songs here and there, and trusting God to provide just enough money to get me by.

As fun and fruitful as my life seemed, it was about to get a *lot* more interesting.

CHAPTER 4

Something There

In the spring of 1999, a friend from Bible college, Jason Duff, invited me to lead worship as part of a weekly Bible study group at Palomar College in San Marcos.

"By the way," he said, "I met this girl named Melissa. She's amazing. You ought to see how much she loves the Lord."

"Cool," I replied, without giving it much thought.

Soon after I showed up at Palomar for the first night, Jason introduced me to Melissa Henning. *Wow*, I thought. *He was right. She is lovely.* But since my friend was the one getting to know her, I didn't think anything beyond that.

I remember leading worship in a circle outside the school. It was *awesome*. As we sang, I looked up and couldn't help but notice Melissa, her arms outstretched, singing with complete abandon. It threw me for a loop, and for a moment I felt like an intruder because of how totally immersed she was in the Lord's presence. I had never seen someone my age with such unabashed passion for God.

Afterward, she and I had an uneventful exchange along the lines of, "It was nice to meet you."

In the coming weeks, I would see Melissa at the Bible study or in other group settings. Jason kept me updated on his interest in her, but as time went on, it became evident that not much was happening on that front. In fact, the more time she and I spent around each other, the more we began to realize there might just be some chemistry between *us*.

I finally called her to talk about it. She agreed that the interest was mutual, but neither of us wanted to do anything to hurt Jason. He was one of my best friends, he was leading the Bible study, and he was still hopeful that sparks would fly with Melissa.

Still, Melissa and I started hanging out a little bit, one on one—meeting for lunch or a cup of coffee and to talk—keeping it quiet at first. She was amazing. We talked for hours about God and music and a lot of other things, and I remember falling in love with her quickly.

When we were together one day, I started thinking: *I have to tell her. I have to tell her.* My palms were sweaty.

"Melissa," I said, "I...want you to know that...I love you."

There was a pause. If you looked up the word "embarrassment" in the dictionary at that moment, you would see a picture of my beet-red face.

Sighing a little, she replied, "Jeremy, I appreciate that, but I can't really tell *you* that right now. For me to say those words would be a pretty huge commitment."

Needless to say, I was devastated. That conversation caused some awkwardness between us for a while, but we kept on getting to know each other. Finally it seemed like the time had come to let Jason know about the budding relationship.

When I told him that I had been seeing Melissa, I felt the tears welling up. "Dude, I'm so sorry," I said. "I don't want to do anything to hurt you."

He didn't say much, but he was bummed. My friends were bummed. Her friends, too. Just about everyone in the Bible study was surprised. It caused friction between Melissa and me, because she thought, *This can't be right if everyone's upset about it.*

In the middle of all of this, Melissa, Jason and I went with a group from Vista's college class on a mission trip to Maui. God did amazing things on that trip. We shared the love of Jesus with some of the poor islanders who live beyond the tourist areas. On the down side, during the trip Melissa broke things off with me. I was crushed. I wound up sobbing like a little kid.

I called my mom to talk it through. "Mom," I said, exasperated. "What's *wrong* with you women?! Why is it all so dramatic? I'm torn up. I really thought she was the one."

My mom graciously resisted the temptation to tell me what's wrong with us *men*. As usual, she listened patiently and redirected the focus back toward God's perspective. "Your only choice is to be patient and trust Him," she said...and I couldn't think of any way to argue the point.

Storm Clouds

Meanwhile, at the end of the summer of 1999, I moved out of Marge's house to share a place with a friend from Vista. I was able to pay my share of the rent while dining on lots of low-cost Ramen noodles, cans of tuna and eggs.

I didn't see Melissa much during this season, although she remained on my mind and heart. In October, I heard from a friend that she had been having stomach pain and was going to have some tests done. I went to visit Melissa on the day of the tests to see how she was doing. It was good to see her, even though it felt a little strange. We were friends, but I was still down about how things had gone between us. Her problem turned out to be a large but non-cancerous cyst, which doctors removed.

Life went on, with Melissa and I staying mostly on separate paths. I recorded my first CD, a 10-song project called *Jeremy Camp: Burden Me.* Jean-Luc produced it, and we recorded it at Horizon Christian Fellowship thanks to pastor Mike MacIntosh. Musically, it felt like God had opened another door, and I was so grateful to Jean-Luc for mentoring and supporting me during this hard time with Melissa. I kept playing music, sometimes with The Kry. I rarely saw Melissa, but that winter I heard she was dealing with stomach pains again.

In the spring of 2000, a friend called with alarming news: "Hey, man, that cyst came back, and they took it out. And it is cancerous." That was the first time the "c" word had reared its ugly head. Even though Melissa and I were only distant friends at that point, my heart felt heavy for her.

I drove to the hospital, about 90 minutes away, almost immediately. Once there, I learned that the diagnosis was ovarian cancer, an aggressive form of the disease. Chemotherapy would be the next step. Melissa's parents, Mark and Junette, were in the room with her when I walked in. They hugged me and then left us alone.

When I saw her, she was smiling from ear to ear—practically glowing. My first reaction was shock. *Why is she so happy? She just found out she has cancer. I would be devastated.*

"How're you doing?" I managed.

She looked at me and said something I'll always remember. "Jeremy, if I were to die from this cancer, and just one person accepted Jesus because of it, it would all be worth it."

Amazing. Her attitude floored me—but it also resonated in my heart. I felt both convicted and filled with peace in her presence. A verse came to mind: "For to me, to live is Christ, and to die is gain."[12] Looking at the joyful glow on Melissa's face, it occurred to me that Paul was talking not just about our gain when we go to heaven, but about the gain of others on earth who could come to Jesus as they watch how we deal with difficulties. Clearly, Melissa was ready to deny herself, take up her cross, and follow Him to see lives touched through her suffering.[13]

As we talked, I saw that she had written down the words of Ginny Owens' song "If You Want Me To" and taped them beside her bed. The last verse of that powerful ballad says: "When I cross over Jordan, I'm gonna sing, gonna shout / Gonna look into Your eyes and see You never let me down / So take me on the pathway that leads me home to You / And I will walk through the valley if You want me to." Melissa was ready to walk through a dark valley if that was the Lord's plan for her, because she knew deep down that He would hold her hand all the way.[14]

As I drove home that night, emotions toward Melissa resurfaced and went deeper than before. I started crying so hard I could barely drive. "Lord, what's going on?" I asked.

---

[12] *Philippians 1:21*
[13] *See Mark 8:34*
[14] *I later had the privilege of getting to know Ginny Owens and telling her how much "If You Want Me To" meant to Melissa and me. The lyrics hold even more meaning in light of the fact that Ginny is physically blind.*

I STILL BELIEVE

And then these words came out: "Lord, if she tells me she loves me, I'll marry her."

It sounded crazy. I don't know why I even said that. I spent most of that night praying for her, weeping, finding myself drawn ever closer to her.

The next day I called my family and explained all that had transpired. My dad was quiet, so I asked him what he was thinking.

"Well, son," he said, "you know if you go down this path, you might end up being with someone you have to take care of for the rest of your life. It won't be easy. Are you prepared to do that?"

I hadn't thought about that, really, but I knew the answer. "Yes," I said, "that would be okay."

Three Little Words

It was May of 2000 when I drove to Melissa's home for a visit. She had begun her first round of chemotherapy in an attempt to eradicate the cancer. I figured she might be in pain or discomfort because of the chemo. On the way to her house, I thought in my heart, *She's gonna tell me she loves me. I know she's gonna say it.*

We greeted at the door, and I walked in and sat down beside her on the couch. After a minute of small talk, she turned more serious.

"Jeremy," she began, "I never knew why it wasn't working between us. I knew how you felt. And I always cared about you so much. But there was this reservation, and I didn't know why. Now I know why. It was God preparing me. He wanted me to be alone with Him for this time coming, because of what I was about to face."

She paused. "I want to show you something."

She pulled out journal entries and pointed to places on the pages where she had prayed for me, and prayed for my wife—whoever she might be.

"I cared about you so much," she continued. "I even met this guy in between us, but when we were hanging out I couldn't stop thinking about you, and about how he *wasn't* you. When I saw you that day at the hospital, after all these months of praying, I knew..."

Her next words hit me like a wave.

"...I love you."

I was shaken to the core. Although I had hoped to hear those words, dreamed of hearing them, had the feeling she would say them, I found myself responding to her in a way that surprised even me.

"This is...scary," I said. "I don't know if I can do this. Please just give me some time."

Now, I know what you might be thinking—especially the ladies: *You can't be serious! This girl just laid her heart bare and expressed her love for you. You had promised God that if she did that, you would marry her. What is your problem?!* If so, I can't blame you. But even though I had made that promise, it all felt so heavy that I needed to process it. This was a huge moment, and I wasn't quite ready to jump into all that might lie ahead. I was thankful that Melissa didn't freak out or get angry. (That would not have been like her, anyway.) She understood where I was coming from, and she graciously agreed to give me as much space as I needed.

Majestic Wisdom

It just so happened that I was about to head to the mountains of Colorado to play several concerts. When I arrived, one of the concert hosts put me up in a quiet, wooded cabin that was perfect for the kind of prayer and reflection I needed. On that trip, I connected with my friend John David Webster, who lived in the Rockies, and explained my uncertainty about Melissa to him. He spoke words of truth that I desperately needed to hear.

"Jeremy," he said, "if you love her with all of your heart, you can't let fear have any place in the matter. You just have to do what God has called you to do. You can't consider the future. Go with where the Lord has you, and trust Him for the rest."

In that little cabin hideaway, I stayed up most of the night, praying and seeking God. I couldn't sleep even if I had wanted to. I remember being tired as I performed the next day, but finding strength to keep going. I felt a little bit like Jacob, wresting with God. I tried to stay focused on the promise, "If any of you lacks wisdom, he should ask God, who gives generously to all without finding fault, and it will be given to him." [15]

So I was asking, almost begging. *What should I do here, Lord? I don't know. Can I do what You are calling me to do? I need wisdom.*

In a nutshell, His answer that came to me was clear: "You've asked Me, son. She has responded to what you asked Me in the way that you hoped she would. What more do you need?" Still, I was afraid, and so I knew that my next step was to cling to the scripture, "Therefore do not worry about tomorrow, for tomorrow will worry about itself. Each day has enough trouble of its own." [16]

---

[15] *James 1:5*
[16] *Matthew 6:24*

One evening, as I sat on a rock watching the sun set over the mountains, I was overcome and broke down crying. There before me was indisputable evidence of God's majesty and grandeur. I began to cry out, "God, you are so big. You are so amazing. You created all that my eyes can see and so much more. You are in control. You are holding the earth steady; surely you will hold me steady. You have the whole world in Your hands. *I will trust You!*"

Having felt the Lord clear away a huge amount of fear and doubt in my heart over those few days in the Rocky Mountains, I headed back to California and returned to Melissa's parents' house to see her. Even while dealing with chemo, she was also studying to become a teacher. As we sat down and began to talk, I could tell that she was having a hard day. Her long, brown hair was starting to thin out because of the medicine, and she was feeling ill. But, as was typical with her, she was keeping quiet about it and instead asked how *I* was doing. She didn't want to let on that anything was bothering her.

Seizing the moment, I looked into her eyes. "Listen, Melissa, if we're going to get married, you're going to have to be able to tell me everything you're going through."

She looked back at me and said, "Married? Are you asking me to marry you?" We both started to cry.

"I love you," I said, "and I see God's hand and His plan in this whole thing, in how He orchestrated it. I see that He brought us together."

It was a pivotal moment. We both took a deep breath and started laughing. Our hearts shared the same sentiment: *Here we are, God. We just have to trust You.*

Melissa and I were now officially engaged. We told our parents with as much laughter and crying as any cou-

I STILL BELIEVE

ple could. Her mom gave us a ring that had belonged to Melissa's grandmother, and we got it sized to fit her hand as an engagement ring. (I still didn't have enough money to buy a new ring.)

The Road Ahead

As we looked toward a wedding, the challenge of chemotherapy persisted. She had a battle to fight, and we weren't sure of the outcome. During this time, I knew it was crucial for us to dig into God's Word and seek His face, both separately and together. One of the scriptures I love the most became a theme for this season of our life together: "You will seek Me and find Me when you seek Me with all your heart." [17]

It was an emotional, sometimes painful time, but it was also a time of growing together in faith. As her hair fell out completely, I started calling Melissa "my beautiful, bald-haired, brown-eyed babe." She was as beautiful to me without hair as she had been with it—and in some ways, even *more* beautiful because we were now preparing to become one.

Believe it or not, we laughed a lot, too. There was real joy in the midst of the sorrow and uncertainty, because joy, as we know, is not based on our circumstances. When it comes from heaven, true joy transcends anything that we might be facing here on earth. Melissa and I were learning to be thankful and content in all circumstances [18] and to let the joy of the Lord be our strength. [19]

---

[17] Jeremiah 29:13
[18] 1 Thessalonians 5:18
[19] Nehemiah 8:10

We went to church together, and, even on her weaker days, she continued to worship the Lord with the same abandon that I had first seen on her face at the Palomar Bible study. The hats and bandanas she wore to cover her hairless head could not distract me from the beauty of her devotion to our God. I found myself convicted more than once about my *own* level of devotion to Him.

Melissa wasn't always filled with joy, of course. There were struggles to endure as well. Discouragement would creep in like a fog and get her down. Nausea would overtake her. On those days, I would ask God to give me what I needed to help lift her spirits.

Like many engaged couples, we talked and dreamed about our future. We even dared to imagine what life might be like with children running around our house. But in the late summer of 2000, a test that Melissa underwent revealed more problems that threatened to dampen our hopes.

As we sat in the doctor's office, he broke the news to us: "We found some cancer on her uterus. That means we're going to have to perform a hysterectomy."

That news hit me like a hard right uppercut. I could tell by the look on Melissa's face that she felt just as disappointed. It was hard for us to consider walking into marriage knowing there was zero chance we could have children. We weren't quite ready to face that kind of reality.

I told the doctor, "I'm going to have people praying around the country and around the world. If you go in for the operation and there's no cancer on her uterus, you won't remove it, right?"

He stared at me and responded with measured words. "Of course we wouldn't," he said, "but we've done the tests… and it's there. I'm sorry."

We sent out a call for intercession, asking everyone we knew (and everyone *they* knew) to lift up Melissa and pray for healing. On the day of the surgery, I paced the hospital floors, praying while friends and family prayed as far as we could spread the word.

"God, You are the healer," I pleaded. "We need Your healing power today. Please heal Melissa."

A little while later, Melissa's mom came running out of her room. "It's gone!" she said. "The cancer is gone. They didn't remove her uterus!"

I fell to my knees right there in the hallway, overwhelmed. "Thank You, God! Thank You!" It was unbelievable. I started calling people and sharing the news, "God healed her! He did it! Thank you so much for praying with us!"

It felt amazing. The cancer was *gone*. There was no trace of it. God had given us a great gift of hope. We didn't have to begin our marriage thinking we couldn't ever have kids. And by that point, we were eager to seal our union and begin our new life together as husband and wife.

CHAPTER 5

Storybook Hopes

O n a mild afternoon, October 21, 2000, Melissa and I were married at Horizon Rancho Santa Fe. By the day of the wedding, things were going decently with her health. She was no longer my bald beauty. She had grown a little bit of spiky hair, and she was stoked about it. We had fun with that.

Among the church full of attendees that day was Jason Duff, the friend who had first introduced Melissa and me. It had taken a while, but we had become friends again. I deeply appreciated his graciousness in supporting Melissa and me on our wedding day.

The worship center was absolutely beautiful, and the atmosphere was filled with the tender presence of the Holy Spirit. My dad performed the ceremony, which made it all the more special. There was definitely a *whole lot* of weeping and crying. Melissa and I sang together the sweet lyrics, "I love You, I love You, I love You…and my heart will follow wholly after You." The presence of God was so thick in that place. It was undeniable that we were there to glorify our King.

Our hearts and minds were firmly rooted in one of my life verses: "However, I consider my life worth nothing to me, if only I may finish the race and complete the task the Lord Jesus has given me—the task of testifying to the gospel of God's grace." [20]

The beauty of the Lord on Melissa's face was truly amazing. She radiated the peace and joy of Christ when she walked down the aisle. I felt like the most blessed man on the planet.

Hawaiian Respite

My new bride and I flew to Oahu, where we stayed at a family member's place for a two-week honeymoon. The only word I can use to describe our getaway was *unbelievable*. All of the drama, the battle with cancer, the called-off hysterectomy, the wedding preparations—all of that seemed to wash away like footprints in the sandy beaches where we walked. We were so thankful to the Lord for this time together. It felt more precious than just a honeymoon. It was a celebration of knowing that God was with us, had seen us through so much already, and would continue to walk with us as we kept our eyes on Him.

During this time of celebration, the Lord gave me a song that expressed the depth of our convictions. I had been reading and thinking about the scripture, "For we walk by faith, not by sight." [21] I still didn't know what awaited Melissa and me in our life together, but things were looking better. We were cautiously bold enough to use the "r" word—remission—in talking about the cancer that we dared to hope was now gone.

....

[20] *Acts 20:24*
[21] *2 Corinthians 5:7*

And so I sat down with my guitar and begin to write the words and music to "Walk By Faith." It came to me in a short time. The lyrics that poured out began with two questions: "Will I believe You when You say, Your hand will guide my every way?" And, "Will I receive the words You say, every moment of every day?" My heart, and Melissa's heart, were filled with faith and trust, and yet I had to inquire honestly of the Lord: Am I really, *really* ready to follow You wherever You lead? No matter what lies ahead?

The chorus expressed my resolve: "I will walk by faith, even when I cannot see, because this broken road prepares Your will for me."

The road that Melissa and I were walking was certainly not a smooth or sunny one. Potholes and uneven pavement marked our course. It was dark and hard to see more than a few feet ahead of us. And yet we were still standing, still moving forward, still clinging to the One who promised to take us through our journey to the other side.

I played the song for Melissa, and we just sat there quietly, soaking it in, feeling thankful for the moment of calm, and for the assurance that the Lord would guide us no matter what the future might hold.

We got a taste of what the immediate future would hold while we were still on our honeymoon. Melissa noticed something going on with her stomach. "It feels weird, like it's swelling," she told me, with concern etched in her eyes. "I don't know why."

We tried to imagine that it was something, anything, *other* than the cancer returning, especially since this was our honeymoon, and we didn't want to give place to the idea. "Maybe it's just indigestion," I said hopefully. That was our mindset. You don't want to think about it. We couldn't do anything until we returned home, anyway.

But we knew that soon after we were back in California, she would need to be tested. The toughest battles loomed just around the bend.

CHAPTER 6

Even when I Cannot See

*F*rom the honeymoon to the hospital—it was the very last thing we wanted to face. But soon after leaving the beauty of Hawaii and returning home, we went in for tests to see what was happening with Melissa's abdomen.

The doctor told us she had some fluid buildup in her stomach that needed to be drained. I held her hand during the procedure, which was a difficult one to watch because it was so painful for Melissa to endure. After they had tested the fluid, the doctor came in and asked if he could speak with me privately. That's hardly ever a good sign.

"What's going on?" I asked him when we reached the hallway.

He was aware that we were newlyweds, and I saw the compassion in his eyes. "I'm afraid the cancer is...well, it's all over her. It has returned, and it has metastasized to other parts of her body. I'm sorry to have to tell you this."

The news hit me hard, but I didn't feel devastated right away. The words of "Walk By Faith" were still fresh in my mind, and I held on to a measure of peace in the midst of this unwelcome message.

"Okay, so what do we do now?" I asked.

He looked at me intently. "No, see, there's nothing else we can do."

"What do you mean?"

"Our treatment options are very few. Jeremy, she probably has weeks or months to live."

At that moment it all hit me harder than before. I started crying. He stood with me quietly. I tried to compose myself. Taking a breath, I walked back into the room where Melissa was, and she just looked at me without saying anything. It was as if she knew. I sat down beside her, and she started crying.

As we drove home that day, Melissa said something that rocked my world. I didn't know why she would speak these words, especially when we were still reeling from the news the doctor had given to us.

"I want to let you know," she said, "that's it's okay if you find somebody else after I go, and I don't want you to have to wait. You don't have to sit in this grief for a long time."

My initial reaction was, "Why are you telling me this? We're in a fight here. I'm still gonna fight." She wasn't giving up, either, but I think she saw the reality that we faced. In line with her other-centered nature, she thought enough to plant a seed that she knew could prove a great help to me in the years to come.

Now, the battle was *on*. Even as we faced the prospect of limited treatment options, we put out the word for prayer among everyone we knew and, once again, asked them to spread the word. Pastors and friends started coming over to the house to pray over Melissa, to anoint her with oil, to worship and praise God in the midst of this storm.

All the while, I was battling a dose of anger toward Him. It was difficult for me to understand why Melissa had been healed during our engagement...but now this? *Lord, why would You give us that hope? Why let us believe things would be okay? But God, I still believe You are in control. Please heal her!*

Still Good

Every three days or so, Melissa would have to go in and have her stomach drained at the hospital. That painful procedure drove home a reality that we could no longer escape. One evening, she was lying on the couch in the living room, moaning in pain, when she asked me, "Can you pull out your guitar, and can we worship?"

I grabbed my guitar and we started singing together. "I cry out for Your hand of mercy, to heal me, 'cause I am weak and I need Your love to free me. O my Rock, my strength in weakness, come rescue me, O Lord. You are my hope, and Your promise never fails me. And my desire is to follow You forever. For You are good, for You are good, for You are good to me..."

I looked up while singing "for You are good" and saw Melissa, with literally every ounce of strength she had, lifting her hands to the Lord. I just broke. How could her mind be so set on worship at this time? It was still unbelievable to me, that kind of unshakeable faith. The depth of her heart continued to amaze me.

Even on the roughest days, she still cried out to the Lord and proclaimed, "You are good. In the midst of the hardships and pain, You are good. Our circumstances don't make sense, but You are good." My dad always has said, "Life is hard, but God is good." Now, Melissa and I hung on to that promise with each passing day and night.

We tried to balance our prayers and hopes for divine healing with the pursuit of every possible avenue of help that the medical/health community had to offer. We flew out to the renowned M D Anderson Cancer Center in Houston, Texas, because we had a connection who could get us an appointment. Our hopes were up, but the doctors there said all they could do was put Melissa on the same chemotherapy that others had recommended...and that it probably wouldn't make much difference.

If you're a follower of the Lord who has walked through a serious illness with a loved one, you probably can relate to the challenge of balancing the divine and the human. We prayed, we believed for healing, we constantly found ourselves refocusing on God's promises. But at the same time, we explored "holistic treatment," made dietary changes, tried garlic soup and other "cancer-fighting" foods. We took these steps while trusting the Lord for healing. We made the effort, battling both in the spirit and in the natural.

One of the hardest things for me was having to stand by, helplessly, as my wife's pain became excruciating. She began to succumb to dehydration. Equipment was brought into the house, and I would change out her hydration pack. I gave her pain medications through an IV tube that went into her arm. I was her primary caregiver, a duty that I was more than willing to perform...except that it gave me a front-row seat to see my beloved wracked with miserable pain.

More than once I thought, *I can't do this anymore*, but God provided just enough strength to get us through the next wave. Along the way, we were still trusting God, still talking about the future, and even still dreaming about the possibility of children. A friend brought us an illustrated children's book one day. We received it as a heartfelt gift and a statement of hope that we could still dare to consider brighter days. We felt encouraged at times like that despite all of the uncertainty.

I was so thankful to have parents who were walking with the Lord during this intense season. My mom called just about every day with another scripture that God had given her to share with us—verses filled with encouragement, exhortation and comfort; reminders of the Lord's goodness in the midst of trials; examples of saints who had walked through fire and emerged with deeper faith in the One who kept them from going up in flames.

Even so, as the days wore on, Melissa lost weight rapidly. Her stomach fluid required frequent draining. Eventually, the pain became more acute. Caring for her at home became increasingly difficult.

It was time to face the unthinkable next step in our journey.

CHAPTER 7

Toward Home

O n New Year's Eve of 2000, I played the song "Walk By Faith"—which I had written on our honeymoon—for the first time in a public setting. Melissa wanted desperately to come to the show. She was in a wheelchair, she was sick, and she was weak. But she summoned the strength to make it there.

As I was singing "hallelujah, hallelujah..." at the end of the song, I looked down and saw my wife in her wheelchair, with her arms outstretched toward heaven and a beaming smile on her face. Just like the first time I had seen her praising God on the night we met, it still blew me away. She was proclaiming, "I know why I'm here on this earth: to worship my God until He brings me home, whenever that may be."

So many friends supported us financially during this season. People gave and gave and gave. I could never thank everyone enough for how selflessly they loved on us. Joey Buran, who was then a pastor at Calvary Chapel Costa Mesa (he was the "California Kid" surfing legend who went on to found Worship Generation), helped by spreading the word about Melissa and our needs.

We knew the time had come for Melissa to leave home and receive round-the-clock care, so we admitted her to Kaiser Permanente Medical Center in San Diego.[22] Soon after we entered the hospital, Melissa's condition worsened. At some point, I heard one of the doctors say that they would do all they could "to keep her comfortable." Something about that phrase struck me as surrendering prematurely, and, in my fatigue and frustration, I got in the doctor's face to argue with him.

"No, we're not just waiting this out!" I said. "Until the last day, we are going to pray for healing, trust the Lord and not give up. We believe that God heals, and I'm *not* going to give up."

The doctor nodded graciously and went back to his work. Melissa and I knew that she was in God's hands. His will would be done—and that could mean her life on earth was nearing its end. But that didn't mean we were going to stop crying out for healing.

I remember doing just that, praying at Melissa's bedside, sleeping on the floor of her room, or falling asleep in the hospital's chapel. Much of those few weeks is a blur. People brought flowers and cards. Visitors filed in to hug us and pray for us. My family was there the whole time, showing their amazing love and praying for me. Friends would bring guitars and play worship songs in the hospital room. Melissa always had praise music playing, and she would sing along until she grew too weak.

----

[22] *We were living north of San Diego at the time, about thirty minutes up Interstate 5 in Encinitas.)*

I STILL BELIEVE

My mom remembers one day when Melissa was espe-cially tired. I looked at Melissa and said, "We're going to beat this." She looked back at me and started singing softly, "Jesus loves me, this I know…" I joined her and we sang the rest of the song together. She lifted her hands weakly, as high as she could. After a minute or two, she fell into a deep sleep.

True to form, Melissa would always ask how visitors were doing when they came to see her. She never complained about the pain she was enduring. She would grip someone's hand as tightly as she could, smile, and tell them how much she appreciated them.

One morning, as my parents sat in the room with her, Melissa said to them, "I want you to know how much I love you both. You are the in-laws I prayed for, and the Lord brought you into my life."

As the level of attention she needed intensified, Melis-sa was moved into a critical care area. Within a few days, she began to slip in and out of consciousness, until she was only awake for brief periods at a time. The hospital staff increased her pain medication to provide more com-fort. Seeing Melissa struggle less with pain made me realize that the doctor's words about comfort had not deserved my harsh rebuke.

Revival Cry

One night as I sat beside Melissa's bed, watching her sleep, the Lord prompted me to go into the open room next door and start reading the psalms with my guitar in my lap. *Psalms* is such a comforting book of the Bible. I especially love David's raw honesty and the fact that he always comes back around to faith. He'll cry out, "God, I'm going through this trial and it hurts! Why is this happening? But...I will trust in Your loving-kindness. You are good. You are merciful. You are with me!"

As I read, God led me to these verses: "Consider my affliction and deliver me, for I do not forget Your law. Plead my cause and redeem me. Revive me according to Your word."[23] That desperate cry resonated in my own heart, and I began to write the song "Revive Me" then and there. After I wrote the chorus and several verses, I went back in and found Melissa awake. I asked if I could sing the song for her. As I sang it, we both began to cry.

"It's beautiful," she said.

Through my tears I replied, "God gave this to me for us right now."

In the hours that followed, Melissa became less responsive and remained unconscious. We could tell that it wasn't looking good. Her body was shutting down.

On February 5, 2001, about ten of us were gathered in her room, weeping and crying out in prayer. Melissa had not responded to anyone for quite a while. At one point Mike MacIntosh, our pastor friend from Horizon church, whispered to me, "Jeremy, I think you need to let her know it's okay, that she can go be with the Lord."

I nodded weakly, knelt beside Melissa and spoke into her ear. "It's okay, love. We'll be fine. Go and be with the Lord."

A few minutes later, both of our moms began to sing a song about heaven. Sitting on each side of the bed, near Melissa's head, they sang, "Heaven is a wonderful place, filled with glory and grace. I want to see my Savior's face..."

[23] Psalm 119:153-154

All of a sudden, Melissa sat straight up and put her hands on each of their mouths, as if to say, "No, I'm not going yet!" She began to get restless. We began to pray. She started tugging at her legs. Then she told us to put the bed rails down. She said she wanted to get up. We told her she couldn't. Just then we realized that God might be healing her and that we needed to let her get up. As we let the rails down, she stood up and looked me in the eyes.

"It's gone. It's gone!" she said. I thought she was having delusions.

"Jeremy," she said, "you have to believe me. It's all gone." Still not comprehending what was going on, I asked her what she meant.

"Are you healed?"

"Yes," she said. "It's all gone."

Everyone in the room began to rejoice. I was hugging Melissa. My brother Jared was standing there hugging us. Melissa's mom and my mom were jumping up and down, embracing each other. Everyone was rejoicing because Melissa was healed.

When we settled down, Melissa insisted she needed to go into the bathroom. We told her she would need to wait until all the tubes were out of her, and then we helped her back into bed. She lay back down with a peaceful look on her face.

I left the room and started calling friends, saying, "I don't know what just happened, but Melissa sat up in bed and said the cancer's gone. I think...maybe God healed her."

As the day progressed, Melissa slept off and on. At times she would sit up and speak, with a glazed looked in her eyes. We assumed it was because she still had a lot of medication in her system and, as it wore off, she would be herself. But, about five hours later, as I walked into the room where she was, it became clear that God was doing something else, something impossible for our mortal minds to grasp. Melissa had drifted back to unresponsiveness, and her vital signs remained paper-thin. She seemed even weaker now. Looking back, I believe the Lord might have been speaking to Melissa's heart that He was about to free her from "this body of death."[24] The cancer would truly be "gone" when she entered His presence. But at the time it seemed strange and confusing.

I left the room and walked next door again, feeling drained. I fell on my face and cried out, "Lord, what is happening?"

————— ❦ —————

[24] *Romans 7:24b*

CHAPTER 8

Letting Go

I'm not exactly sure how many minutes had passed when one of the friends gathered next door peeked into the room where I lay sprawled on the floor—crying out to God, weeping and longing—and called me back to Melissa's hospital bed.

"Jeremy," he said softly, "it's time."

I rose and started walking back toward her room, crying all the way. I couldn't believe it, but I knew: The moment had arrived to say goodbye to my wife.

My brother Jared, who was then 14, was standing with me, along with my parents, as I began to walk toward Melissa's room. This is a blur, but my mom remembers that Jared looked at me with disbelief in his eyes and embraced me, shaking his head and weeping.

"It's not over," he said. "She's not gone yet."

As we stood together, it occurred to me that Jared's budding faith in God might depend on whatever reassurance his family could offer him in this moment. I grabbed him and looked right into his eyes. "Whatever you do, don't you ever stop serving Jesus. Just because we live in a sick, sin-filled world doesn't mean He's not in control."

Entering her room, my legs buckling, I barely made it across the floor before falling into bed beside Melissa. Worship music was playing in the background. I hugged her and told her I loved her.

Her sister, Heather, spoke in a tearful whisper. "She's with Jesus now."

It was true. She was gone. I dropped to the floor and curled into a ball beside Melissa's bed. Her family began to worship the Lord, raising their hands and singing along as the music played on the CD player. My parents joined in as well—first my mom, and then my dad. The room was filled with singing. I had no desire to move, but at that moment, God spoke gently but clearly to my heart.

"I want you to stand up and worship Me."

My first response was to resist Him. *O God...no, I don't want to stand up and worship right now. There's nothing in me that can do that!*

My mom recognized the struggle going on in my spirit and soul as I lay on the floor. She said to me, in a voice filled with love and resolve, "Honey, you have to lift your hands, you have to worship the Lord."

I felt myself slowly rising from the floor. I knew that I had no choice but to trust my Lord. Even in the most painful, crushing times, He is still worthy to be praised. Praising Him still strengthens us. And praising Him is still a signal to the enemy of our souls that he cannot, will not triumph, even when it might look like he has. God's command to me was actually a loving message from His heart.

My parents helped me to stand. I raised my hands as the music played. Everyone else in the room started raising their hands and worshipping the Lord as well.

It was a powerful moment. As we wept and sang, we felt the presence of God like I never had before. Melissa's lifeless body lay on the bed, but we knew that she, too, was worshipping. She was now before her King. She was free of pain and suffering. The reality of that truth washed over us and made the moment even sweeter.

After a few minutes, my dad and a friend literally carried me out of the room. I was completely spent, as were the rest of my family and Melissa's family.

Present with the Lord

The memorial service a few days later was truly a celebration of Melissa's brief, but monumental, life. Her friends and family shared stories of her deep passion for God— a passion that not even the viciousness of cancer could quench. Among the many words of comfort spoken at the service and during those several days of grieving, I will always remember what Jean-Luc, my dear brother-in-faith, told me.

"My friend, this is why we need to hasten the day," he said. "Let's hasten the day. Jesus is coming back."

That truth rings in my head to this day. "Yes, let's go," I remember saying to him, with a feeling of resolve penetrating the sharp pain. "Let's go and be surrendered to the Lord for the rest of our days."

Growing up, you never think that when you've just turned 23 years old, you'll deal with the heartbreak of saying goodbye to your wife and staying behind while she goes to be with the Lord. But this was my reality. I would face it the only way I knew how: clinging to God like a ship-wrecked sailor clinging to a rock in the midst of a sea of crashing waves beating against him.

I had no idea yet just how strong that Rock would be.

CHAPTER 9

If only One Person

At Kaiser Permanente Medical Center, one of the nurses assigned to Melissa was watching and listening to all that went on in those final days. She took note of the prayer and praise, the tears and hugs, the undying faith that was so evident in Melissa's demeanor.

Seeing all of that caused the nurse to look at her own life. Something was missing. She didn't have a relationship with God, but she came to see how much she wanted and needed one.

Melissa had been praying for her, and others had been praying as well.

A few days before the end, Melissa's father had the opportunity to pray with the nurse and lead her to a saving faith in Jesus Christ.

The powerful words that Melissa had spoken to me almost a year earlier remained fresh: "...if I were to die from this cancer, and just one person accepted Jesus because of it, it would all be worth it."

We were able to tell Melissa this great news while she was still lucid enough to grasp its full meaning.

"Remember that 'one person'?" I told her as we both began to weep with joy at the knowledge that another soul had come into God's kingdom. "This is just the beginning. There will be many more."

PART 2

CHAPTER 10

This Broken Road

A few days after the memorial service, I went back to Indiana to be near my family for a while. Because it was late February, the trees were bare, the ground was dormant, the days were short and the nights were long. The prevailing feeling that gripped me was *numbness*. I felt barely able to rise each day and face the pain and confusion. I tried to talk with God, but the signal between us seemed weak. The idea of playing or writing music was far from my mind as I walked around in a fog.

It was in the midst of my raw sadness that God spoke very clearly to my heart one morning: "Pick up your guitar. I have something for you to write."

"Pick up my...what?"

I don't hear God speaking to me audibly, and I don't always hear His voice prompting me as clearly as I would like. But in the days, weeks and months following Melissa's passing, I heard Him "speaking" in my heart a lot more than I ever had before. Looking back, I believe the Lord was reminding me that He is very near to the brokenhearted.[25] Also, I think God knew how numb I was, how incapable I was of seeing things clearly, and how desperately I needed the clarity and guidance that only He could bring.

In this particular moment, my honest, gut-level response was to argue with God. "No, Lord...no. The *last* thing I want to do is play my guitar!"

After trying to avoid His voice for a quite a while and occupy myself with other tasks, I realized that this strong directive was not going to fade away. In fact, it was growing stronger. Reluctantly, with what little energy I could manage, I picked up my guitar and started playing some chords. Sometimes obedience to the Lord's prompting—even when it's not the most wholehearted obedience at first—brings about a startling change. This was one of those moments. Tears began to flow as I played, and so did the words and notes that would become the song "I Still Believe." The words were a looking glass into how I was feeling:

Scattered words and empty thoughts
seem to pour from my heart
I've never felt so torn before
seems I don't know where to start
But it's now that I feel Your grace fall like rain
from every fingertip, washing away my pain

[25] Psalm 51:17

(Chorus)
I still believe in Your faithfulness
I still believe in Your truth
I still believe in Your Holy Word
even when I don't see, I still believe

Though the questions fog up my mind
with promises I still seem to bear
Even when answers slowly unwind
it's my heart I see You prepare
But it's now that I feel
Your grace fall like rain
from every fingertip, washing away my pain

The only place I can go is into Your arms
where I throw to You my feeble prayers
In brokenness I can see that this was Your will for me
Help me to know You are near...

In these words I was crying out, "God, I don't understand. I'm scattered. I'm broken. The fog is so thick that I can't even see my own hand in front of my face. And yet... even in the middle of all of this pain and hurt, I *do* feel Your grace. I *do* sense Your hand of mercy. I still believe You are here with me, even if the pain in my heart is making it so difficult to feel Your presence. No matter what, Lord, You *are* faithful. You are *faithful*. *You* are faithful. I will believe that."

Pressed But Not Crushed

One line in the song—"Though the questions fog up my mind, with promises I still seem to bear..."—was really difficult to write and to think about. I often wondered if the weight of grief bearing down might crush me, especially as I wrestled with so many promises Melissa and I had held onto. We had thought she would be healed, that our future together would be bright. We had come through a shadowy forest of doubt and had arrived at what we hoped, believed and trusted would be a clearing of sun-drenched hope. Because of that journey from sickness to health back to sickness, I was confused, and I had to be honest with God. If He was going to speak to me so clearly, I definitely felt my heart and mind bursting to respond.

"I don't get it, God!" I cried, continuing to play my guitar. "What do I make of all of this?" As I prayed and questioned and wept, the bridge of the song poured forth from the deepest recesses of my heart: "In brokenness I can see / that this was Your will for me."

This was Your will for me.

I was a little bit surprised to hear those particular words come out. Was it, really? Could it have been His will for Melissa to suffer and go home so young, with so much in front of her? I wasn't sure how to look at it. Did the Lord simply allow her passing to happen as a consequence of life in a broken, sinful world, or could it actually have been something He orchestrated as a part of His will? If it were the former scenario, I had to wonder *why* God would allow it. Couldn't He have stopped her suffering and healed her?! If it were the latter, then it seemed far too painful to grasp on this side of heaven that God's will would include such a wrenching twist.

As I grappled with this deep question, it became apparent to me why some people slip into a place of blaming God for "taking away" a loved one. It certainly can feel that way. I could see myself going that direction if I weren't very, very careful. The last thing I wanted was to become bitter and turn away from God. Even as I asked tough questions of Him and longed for better answers than the ones that seemed to be available at the time, I knew deep down that I would have to find rest in the fact that some things will not make sense until we get to heaven.

A deeper revelation was coming into my heart that the present world is not our home. Heaven was becoming more real to me, and eternal things were becoming clearer than ever before in my life. And I've never been the same since.

This command in the Word came into focus: "Since, then, you have been raised with Christ, set your hearts on things above, where Christ is seated at the right hand of God. Set your minds on things above, not on earthly things. For you died, and your life is now hidden with Christ in God. When Christ, who is your life, appears, then you also will appear with him in glory." [26]

Ultimately, it wasn't critically important that I know *why* Melissa had gone home just when it seemed like the horizon stretched out before us. My only option was to believe that my Savior knows the end from the beginning, knows that we will experience pain in this mortal life, knows we dwell in a sick world, and comes to us during our darkest hours to bring comfort, strength and understanding.

....

[26] *Colossians 3:1-4*

After all, even with the many wonderful things God promises us in His word, He never promises that we won't face trials as we go about our life on earth. In fact, Jesus stated clearly, "I have said these things to you that in me you may have peace. In the world you will have tribulation. But take heart; I have overcome the world."[27] Tribulation was a given—as Melissa and I had discovered firsthand. But because of all the scorn and ridicule and torment that Jesus went through, He was able to overcome the world and give us the gift of true peace.

We're bound to encounter tests, challenges and pain in "this present age," but it's good for us to remember that He has overcome all of that. In the end, through Christ, we are victorious over death.[28] And in the meantime, He remains our refuge, fortress, shield, strong tower, deliverer and strength.

So Torn

In those chilly days in Indiana, my parents were still as incredibly supportive as they had been during Melissa's illness. My mom, a true "warrior of the Word," spoke the truth to me in love through the Scriptures. She gently reminded me every day—sometimes several times a day—of truths that felt like medication being carefully applied to an open wound: that our Lord is a God of comfort,[29] that He would sustain me through this valley of sorrow,[30] that I could trust Him as my loving, caring, close-at-hand Heavenly Father

---

[27] John 16:33
[28] 1 Corinthians 15:55
[29] Isaiah 40:1
[30] Psalm 23

even when my emotions might not line up with the reality of His presence.[31]

For my mom, the words of Hebrews 11 had been particularly comforting in the days after Melissa passed. Sometimes referred to as "Hall of Faith chapter," this portion of Scripture records a list of heroes and heroines who walked by faith and trusted the Lord for different promises, even when they did not see His promises fulfilled in their own lifetimes.

One day she told me, "Jeremy, I don't understand why God gave us those promises, but I feel like He's telling us, just as it says in Hebrews 11:39, that though we were given the promises, we didn't receive what had been promised, but we were to walk by faith. And this would be a deeper kind of faith."

My dad, too, was right there with me. I can remember several times when he would hug me and hold on tight while I cried. Once, we were singing worship songs together, and I broke down. "She was such a worshipper," I said to him, and he embraced me as I wept. I felt thankful to have a father who loved God and loved me with such tenderness.

It was difficult to leave Indiana and head back to California, but I knew it was time to face the reality of life without Melissa in the place where I believed the Lord wanted me to be. The ache in my soul remained raw as I walked through the first days and weeks back on the West Coast in the early spring of 2001.

Friends surrounded me with love, compassion and practical expressions of caring. In that way, I was truly blessed. Even so, I went through the full range of emotions that we humans tend to experience after the passing of a close loved

---

[31] Psalm 42:5,11

one. The initial numbness turned to deep sadness for a while, but as time wore on, I found myself mostly filled with anger. I was mad that Melissa was gone, mad that a life together that had scarcely begun was now over, mad that all we had hoped for seemed to have ended so abruptly.

One day, as I tried to read my Bible, I came to a passage describing one of Jesus' healing miracles. The words on the page stopped me cold. I picked up the Bible in a rage and threw it across the room, where it crashed into the wall and thudded to the floor.

"Why, Lord!?" I cried. "Why didn't you heal my wife? I had faith. I believed. *Why?!*"

I sank back down into my chair in a heap, breathing heavily, eager to put my fist through the nearest wall. As I tried to calm down, I heard the Lord again, speaking to my heart. The message I sensed Him giving me didn't make sense at first, but there was no mistaking it. He was saying, "You're not supposed to know why. That is not My purpose for you. I want you to have a testimony of walking by faith."

Although I heard what He was saying, my response was not immediate acceptance. I was still steamed.

"That is *not* what I want to hear, Lord!" I shouted out. "I want to understand!"

Later on, His words that day would become very real and purposeful—just like many other words God speaks to us that don't seem to make perfect sense when we first hear them.

Please don't get me wrong. I didn't walk around enraged all day long. The emotion came in spurts. And even as I dealt with anger, I also knew that my Heavenly Father was lovingly walking me through this fragile time. Slowly, small doses of healing began to take place. It certainly didn't happen in

I STILL BELIEVE

giant leaps, or even in normal paces. It was baby steps, for sure. But I felt Him empathizing with me. His patience was real. He grieved with me while still knowing the greater purpose of what I was enduring.

When Jesus Mourned

On another morning, the Lord led me to spend some time studying John 11:1-43, where we find Lazarus, the brother of Jesus' friends Mary and Martha, sick and dying in the town of Bethany.

By this point, Mary and Martha knew that Jesus was capable of performing miracles, so they sent for Him to come and heal Lazarus. Jesus eventually came to Bethany, but He didn't get there until Lazarus had already been "dead" and in the tomb for four days. When Jesus arrived, neither one of the two women was happy to see Him. Martha confronted Him and asked why He had not come any sooner. She seemed hurt, confused and even angry. (I could relate!) *If only you had been here, Lord, our brother would still be with us. If only...*

Jesus looked into Martha's eyes and reminded her, "I am the resurrection and the life. He who believes in me will live, even though he dies; and whoever lives and believes in me will never die. Do you believe this?"

Do you believe this? It wasn't just a question for Martha. It was a question for anyone who might ever have cause to doubt whether the Lord was willing to heal in a given situation. It was a question that *I* was wrestling with every hour of every day. Would I continue to believe that He was the resurrection and the life...and that Melissa was more "alive" now than she had ever been on earth?

As the passage goes on, we discover that it wasn't callousness or indifference that had kept Jesus from arriving sooner and healing Lazarus. Because Jesus was "God made man," He felt every emotion you or I could ever feel. He loved, He rejoiced, He seethed (remember the money changers in the temple?), and of course He suffered. And so the Word tells us that when He saw where Lazarus had been buried, "Jesus wept." [32]

The original word for "wept" is a strong one there. It's not just shedding a few tears. It basically means convulsing out of a depth of sorrow that shakes you to the core of your being. It's about as overcome with mourning as a person can get.

Why did Jesus weep? Knowing the whole story now, it might seem strange to us that He did so. Again, being "God made man," He had to be aware that there was a greater purpose and a "happy ending" on the way. (In this case, it would be Lazarus rising from the dead and walking out of the tomb.) So why cry? I think a big part of the reason is because Jesus *loved* Lazarus, and He loved Mary and Martha, and He knew they were hurting. I believe His tears were, at least in some measure, a sign that He was empathizing with their pain as they grieved—identifying with these precious ones who had experienced a searing loss.

The Savior graciously did the same for me. I felt Him weeping with me at times. Even in my outbursts of anger and questioning—*if only, Lord!*—He didn't withdraw from me. And even when I couldn't take a step forward, He didn't rush me. A sense of peace began to make its way back into the

---

[32] John 11:35

recesses of my heart. I still battled and asked hard questions, but the prevailing sense was that I was not alone.

Ryan and Pastor Jon

God also brought key people into my life at just the right time to serve as agents of healing. A little more than a month had passed since the memorial service when Melissa's brother, Ryan Henning, and I packed our bags for a road trip from Southern California up to Oregon, driving in Ryan's truck. Along the way, we just kind of hung out. We had an amazing time. Sometimes we cried as we thought of the void left by the passing of his sister and my wife. At other times, we were quiet. It was a good time to get away. But we also had a destination in mind.

We were going to see the pastor who had been instrumental in leading me to Christ back at youth camp the summer before my junior year of high school. Pastor Jon Courson had been the main speaker at that camp, challenging us to live fully surrendered lives to Jesus. After Melissa's passing, my parents had encouraged me to contact him and see if we could connect. I knew that he been through a trial even more severe than what I was walking through. Jon Courson had lost his wife in a car accident, leaving him with three small children. Later, he would lose one of those children, a teenage daughter, in another car accident. Two of the dearest people in his life had gone home to be with the Lord within a span of about twelve months. Jon had graciously invited Ryan and me to visit his home.

As we got closer to our arrival, I felt a sense of anticipation mingled with uncertainty. For the most part I was eager to see Jon and hopeful that he could shed light on some of my questions about Melissa's passing. When we got to his home, he put us up in a little cabin on the property. I was thankful that he had welcomed us so warmly.

On the first day of our visit, as we were talking, I realized I had so much to ask him. Here was a man who had been where I was, basically, and who was living life "down the road" from it. I saw a depth of compassion in his eyes that could only come from knowing exactly what I was dealing with. He also had a way of putting me at ease. One of the first questions I asked him was about the trial Melissa had been allowed to endure.

"There was so much pain," I said. "What about that? Why did she have to suffer like that? She loved the Lord. We did everything we could. We prayed, we believed. I just don't understand it."

Jon must have known how exhausted I was from the struggle of grief, because his answer was filled with kindly wisdom.

"Jeremy, you can rest your head on your pillow at night, knowing you did all that you could. This was God's plan. He heard your prayers. He comforted Melissa. Rest, knowing that you *did* seek the Lord in obedience." Those words washed over me like a balm of much-needed encouragement.

As the conversation continued, Jon turned to the Scriptures for inspiration. "Remember after the Israelites crossed the Red Sea, and Miriam was playing her song of celebration on the tambourine?" he asked me.

"Yes," I replied, picturing the image of Miriam dancing and praising in triumph as the Hebrews reached the other shore of the sea safely, out of reach of the Egyptian army.[33]

---

[33] *The whole account is laid out in Exodus chapters 14 and 15.*

I STILL BELIEVE

"Well," he said, "she missed out on the depths of how God could have used her."

"Missed out? What do you mean?" I asked, thinking that Miriam was one of the heroes of the story.

"What she did, she really should have done earlier," Jon said. "Granted, I wasn't there, but when they were all assembled *before* crossing the Red Sea, not knowing what to do, she could have been singing and praising the Lord on *that* side as well—not just afterward."

I could see his point. It's easy to forget that before the Red Sea crossing, everything seemed hopelessly lost for the Israelites. They were pinned against a raging abyss by a bitterly vengeful Pharaoh and his bloodthirsty army—an army ready to pounce on this ragtag band of Hebrews who were running for their lives from a land of slavery.

Jon reminded me that even in those circumstances, "We still need to worship our God. He's still in control. It's easy *after* we've tasted God's deliverance and seen His miracles to say, 'Yes, Lord, you are the best!' But it's tough when you don't see any outcome, or any good, in a really dark time, to say, 'God, You are good. You are good. No matter what, You are good.'"

That reminder would stick with me for a long time. It was hard to hear it, but I knew Jon was on to something. God was, is and always will be worthy of praise and adoration, regardless of our circumstances. I was still hurting, and I'm sure the pain and desperation were evident in my eyes. But Jon's words pierced through a little bit of the fog. He didn't sugarcoat the truth or try to provide easy answers.

"We'll probably never fully understand suffering until we're in the presence of the Lord for eternity," he said.

The Bigger Picture

To help bring the concept of suffering into sharper focus, Jon walked Ryan and me through a vivid word-picture: When a caterpillar gets into its cocoon and is writhing to get out to become a butterfly, you can see the struggle unfolding. It's tempting to want to "help" the little guy get out of the cocoon. But if you try to relieve the pressure and free it before the right time, the creature won't develop into a butterfly. It will die without having fully matured. In a similar way, the "beauty" of our lives often must emerge from a season of struggle to be truly beautiful. Strength and maturity arise out of a cradle of pain.

Jon did a good job of cushioning the blow of the truth he was sharing with me. "Jeremy, I know it doesn't make sense, but that is a part of the bigger picture. Through the suffering, God has a greater purpose. In heaven now, Melissa's reward is *great*. If we can look at things from an eternal perspective, we can see that her reward is so much greater than any earthly suffering."

He invited me to play a song at his church's Sunday-night service. I was appreciative but extremely reluctant. "I think it would be good for you," he offered, "because at your greatest depth of pain, God will use you to have the greatest impact."

That night, I played and sang "I Still Believe" as part of the service. Really, I pretty much wept through it and then spoke briefly about Melissa's passing. I can't remember exactly what I said, but I remember the compassion on the faces of the congregation. It was a painful but powerful night. I sensed God's hands holding me up as He used my agony to speak a word of cling-to-faith truth to a group of fellow worshippers.

As Ryan and I left the Courson home and headed back to California, I felt a glimmer of hope. All was not quite well with my soul, but the healing process had begun. I was deeply thankful that God had used the man who led me to a renewed faith in Christ when I was a teenager to speak such comfort to my heart now.

I Will Yet Praise Him

As spring turned into summer, I was asked to sing "I Still Believe" in lots of different settings. Many times I would find myself crying out beforehand, "Lord, I don't *feel* like worshiping You today. I don't *feel* like saying 'I still believe.'" But when I went out to sing, God would hold me up, and the impact on the listeners would be even greater than I could have anticipated. People would cry as they sang along on the chorus or just let the words wash over them. It was so incredibly clear to me that *God* was moving and ministering in those moments. It had *nothing* to do with me. Most of the time, I didn't want to sing the song! I was struggling to believe the words that were coming from my lips. I just had to be honest with the Lord—He knew I was a reluctant participant in the whole thing—and let Him do what He wanted as I shared the music.

My journey truly was just beginning, though. I had my share of really rough days. Different triggers would release a rush of emotions: watching a movie with some kind of grief in it—I remember weeping in the theater during a war movie—seeing a young couple holding hands and laughing together, noticing a mom and dad playing with a child at a park. Worse than any of that, I felt my heart starting to get a little bit hard. Anger and coldness slipped back in as if they wanted to stay a while. I didn't like it, but I sensed that facing the anger welling up from within would be a necessary part of the grieving process.

At the same time, things were picking up musically. I began playing and singing more, mostly leading worship in churches around Southern California. I would push past the anger, step out front and do my thing—sing, talk about the Lord, witness—but then, often, I would slip back into the hardness.

Looking back, I can see why some people in my life at the time wondered if I might be jumping into music ministry too quickly, not allowing enough time to truly grieve the passing of my wife. I really think I *was* grieving, but I also felt God gently pushing me, saying, "I'll take care of you. You just go ahead, walk into what I'm doing." He knew that writing songs, and then sharing the music that poured out of my heart, would play an important role in my healing *and* in encouraging others.

As more people responded to "I Still Believe" and "Walk By Faith" when I played them, it seemed like the time to record the songs so they could be shared more widely. A friend told me about Adam Watts and Andy Dodd, two young producers. I heard their stuff and liked it, so I called them about the possibility of recording a demo. I told them what was going on in my life. "It's a hard time, but I need to get these songs out," I said. They agreed without hesitation.

We went into a studio and recorded "Walk By Faith" first. As we were working on the final mixes of the song, I got a strong feeling that the Lord was going to use it to speak into the lives of others who were going through painful trials. A sense of gratitude washed over me that day, and I prayed, "Thank you, Lord, that you might use what

I STILL BELIEVE

Melissa and I have gone through to help others in their own struggles."

I knew my heart still needed to be softened before the next chapter of life could begin. With that desire at the forefront of my mind, I made plans to get away to the mountains for a few days of prayer and fasting.

CHAPTER 11

Breaking My Fall

*I*n the fall of 2001, I drove several hours to a little mountain cabin and collapsed in my room, worn down and hungry for inspiration from the Lord.

My prayer for this time away was basically, "God, I need a breakthrough. I feel like You are doing something, and I don't want to miss it. I can't stumble through my days numb or hardhearted. I want my heart to be soft and pliable."

For three days, I mostly stayed in the one-room cabin, praying, fasting and playing my guitar. The time passed more slowly than I had expected, and it was just...hard. I thought some big revelation would land on me, that I would hear the Lord's voice and feel a major change happen during these days away. I was ready to weep. But my heart and mind refused to budge. I couldn't shake the questions and confusion that hung low on my soul like a fog. Tears would not flow, and hardness remained. This funk was expressed in music and lyrics I wrote while at the cabin that would become the song "Breaking My Fall." Writing and playing guitar had become my most precious "release valves" during this season, and that comes through in the song:

(Verse 1)
So easily I fall, so easily You reach Your hand out,
Quickly will I drown, know the pulls of all my reason,
So easily will I feel, so easily will Your peace surpass me,
Quickly will I trust in anything I think is worthy
How many times You make the waves calm down,
So I won't be afraid now

(Chorus)
I saw You breaking my, breaking my fall, what am I
supposed to do? (2x)

(Verse 2)
How precious are Your thoughts
And many that You think about me,
Faithful are Your ways,
I always feel Your grace abounding,
Quickly will I call, quickly will You answer my cry,
Carefully will You bring, everything I need in my life,
How many times You make the waves calm down,
So I won't be afraid now

(Bridge)
This narrow road I'm walking,
this world will try to draw,
Your Word will help me fight it, with You I'll face it all

The main question in the song—What am I supposed to do?—summed up exactly how I felt as I continued seeking the Lord during these few days in the mountains. But the lyrics also contained words expressing my faith that somehow, some way, God would bring deliverance from the pain: "Quickly will I call, quickly will You answer my cry." The only problem was that my definition of "quickly" wasn't lining up with the Lord's.

On the third morning, as I left the cabin to break my fast with a meal, I was feeling bummed out. I prayed, "Lord, my heart's desire was to have a huge revelation, weeping in Your presence, feeling Your healing touch—something momentous. I don't understand why nothing has changed."

As I drove back down the mountain toward home, I must have looked like a zombie to any oncoming drivers who noticed me as we passed each other. But at some point along the way, I slipped my recently recorded demo CD into the player to see how it sounded. When "Walk By Faith" came on and I heard the words that God had given me during that bittersweet time on my honeymoon with Melissa, it was as if the sun suddenly pierced through the clouds on a cold, damp day. Warmth suddenly penetrated my heart, melting the ice that had built up. At long last—or so it seemed to me—the tears began to flow.

The floodgates opened, and pent-up emotions rushed out. I was so overcome that I had to pull the car over, bury my head in my hands and weep...and weep...and weep. It hit me, more than before, exactly what the song was saying.

"Okay, Lord," I said, through tears, "I can't see, but I *will* walk by faith. I don't understand, but I know there's a greater plan. It will be okay. You will make it okay." Those few minutes of release at the end of the time away ushered in a new season. A great deal of healing started coming about in the days and weeks that followed my ride home that morning.

Finally, as my heart grew softer, I felt myself praying with more hope and expectancy, saying things like, "Here I am, God. Let's do this. It's time to live. I'm broken, but whatever You want me to do, I'm willing."

The Beauty I Hear

Another song that God gave me later spoke to some of the same things I was feeling and thinking as He began to heal my heart. "When You Are Near" touched on the reality of redemptive hope in the midst of pain:

(Verse 1)
There's no need to say a thing
When I'm before You
In this silence I feel refreshed with peace
Break this noise that binds the voice that tries to speak
Open up my eyes to see Your gracious sovereign reach

(Chorus)
It's hard to talk when I feel that You are near,
When all is quiet it's the beauty that I hear
This hidden place where I know that You've calmed my fears,
I know that You've washed my tears

(Verse 2)
The seasons of change I've faced have never

> *left me wounded*
> *Only scars of hurt but never deeply rooted*
> *This healing I have felt no burden can replace*
> *Redemptive hope has been the story of my pain*
>
> *(Bridge)*
> *All is lost without the breath of life You give*
> *And You give so much*
> *I want nothing more than You, so here's my heart*

I had wounds from the pain, but God was beginning to heal them. I still had scars that would always be there, but I could look at them through the lens of hope.

In December of 2001, I received an e-mail from a record-company representative named Tyson at BEC Recordings. "We've been hearing a lot about you from a friend, and we would like to talk with you. Do you have a demo you could send?" he wrote.

As it happened, I had spent some time with the head of the label, Brandon Ebel, at Cornerstone music festival when I was a 14-year-old kid camping out with my family. Small world!

I mentioned that connection to Tyson in my response to his e-mail. "Dude, this is awesome," he replied. The CD got from me to Tyson to Brandon, who called me a few days later.

"Bro, what's going on?" he said. "How is your family in Indiana?"

I told him the whole story of Melissa's passing. He was shocked and expressed his condolences. After a pause, he added, "These songs, oh my goodness. There is a lot here. I'd really like to work with you."

Naturally, I was excited about the possibility, but after all that had happened I knew what my immediate answer would be.

"I need to pray about this," I told Brandon. "I've been through a lot, and I need to make sure every decision is from God." He totally understood and encouraged me to take my time.

While I was considering the next steps, Brandon asked me one day, "What about doing this worship project once a year, called *Any Given Sunday?*" That really piqued my interest because of my love for leading worship. We agreed for me to start working on that project first.

In the midst of that project, the Lord provided strong confirmation that the time was right to record my own songs with BEC. This was rooted in my increasing desire to proclaim God's faithfulness while extending comfort to others, just as I was receiving comfort.[34]

I signed a contract with BEC in May of 2002 and recorded two albums, *Stay* and *Carried Me*, right in a row, all in the course of about a month. (For *Stay*, we actually used five out of the six songs from the demo I had sent to Tyson earlier.) It was an amazing, whirlwind time, but it felt good to be putting these songs into a form that would allow them to reach more people with a message of hope.

Word Spreading

With the release of these two albums, the word began to get around about my music and, more important, about

---

[34] *Paul talks about this in 2 Corinthians 1.*

my testimony of what the Lord was bringing me through. As a result, I was invited to join a bunch of other Christian artists on the 2002 edition of the Festival Con Dios tour, which included a number of well-known singers and bands, along with booths, events and shows such as motocross demonstrations. It was a high-energy happening, and it would travel to cities throughout the United States.

You might think this kind of news would blow my mind—and you would be right. It was *totally* mind-blowing! Here I was asked to go out on my first tour, and the artists on the bill included TobyMac, Mercy Me, Audio Adrenaline, Out of Eden, Pillar, The Benjamin Gate, Sanctus Real, Tree 63 and Everyday Sunday. *Wow.* I had been listening to these artists and their music, and now I had the privilege of ministering *with* them. I couldn't help it; I was so excited.

I remember praying after confirming plans to join the tour, "O God, I can't believe I get to go out around the country and share with so many people about what You're doing. Thank you!" I experienced such a pure feeling of anticipation as the start of the tour drew nearer. Once it kicked off, I would share my testimony every night, play "I Still Believe" (among other songs), and lay out the story behind the song.

As the tour continued and my songs reached a larger audience through CDs, a wave of stories from listeners began to build. People would write, e-mail, or come up to me and tell me they had walked through cancer with someone close to them: their wife, or their son, or their parent. Others would tell me about the passing of a loved one and how much the words in the songs resonated with them. These stories were so meaningful to me because they confirmed one of the promises that the Lord had made to me in the deepest places of hurt: that He had a plan and a purpose far beyond what I could have seen at first.

My merchandise table during Festival Con Dios was close to the table where a South African band, The Benjamin Gate, had its music and other merch for sale. From week to week, as I started getting to know many of the other acts on the tour, one member of the Gate in particular became a new friend with whom I felt increasingly comfortable talking.

CHAPTER 12

Something New

NOTE TO THE READER: In this chapter, Jeremy welcomes a new voice to help him tell the story from another perspective. Look for the name and the indented words, and you'll see what we mean.

P eople who know me well—and even those who have only been around me for a few minutes—can tell that I tend to be really outgoing. Add to my natural personality bent the fact that I was so stoked to be on the festival tour in the fall of 2002, and it's no surprise that I spent most of the time during the tour making new friends among my fellow artists. It was incredible. I must have looked like a kid on Christmas morning, walking around with a big smile on my face.

I found myself praying often, "God, I'm amazed at how You have brought me from all of that pain to this place of open doors, allowing me to minister these songs and share Your words...thank You so much."

While waiting my turn and watching the other artists perform, I had noticed a red-haired girl on stage rocking it out with her band. I found out that her name was Adrienne Liesching, or Adie for short, and that she was part of The Benjamin Gate. My first impression was that she must be a loud, hardcore rocker chick. But when I introduced myself to her after a show, she surprised me with a mellow, sweet "Hello." And as we talked, she seemed to have a quieter spirit than I had anticipated based on the way she performed on stage.

Because her band's table was near mine, we started hanging out a lot during the early part of the tour and became fast friends. It was incredibly easy to talk with her. She had heard about my testimony, and she would ask me questions about Melissa: "What was she like? How did you first meet? Tell me about her walk with the Lord." I liked that she felt so comfortable asking me personal questions. She was genuinely inquisitive.

ADIE: ....

I had not watched Jeremy play yet. I had heard through the grapevine that this new guy's wife has passed on not long before. They said he's this godly man and you've got to hear his story. I was intrigued by the line of people at his table after he played. It was more than the other bands'. Having been in the industry for a couple of years, I was like, hmm, what's the story here? I had become disheartened by the Christian-music scene, so I was curious about someone who had gone through such a painful trial and was standing strong on the other side. I could tell he was standing strong just by his demeanor. I wanted to know more about someone who seemed to be living what he said, and I wanted to know more about Melissa. How could one person touch so many hearts? What was her take on God? It seemed so deep and real, and I was desperately hungry for it. Jeremy was very encouraging to me when I asked.

Adrienne would hear me talk about the Lord and say, "Tell me more. What do you mean by that? How does that work?" It looked to me as if she was feeling kind of burned out and seeking something fresh. The Benjamin Gate had been playing and traveling for several years, doing the daily grind, far from their home in South Africa, and she was away from her family. It was rough enough being young and on tour, much less doing so in a "strange land" without many of the comforts of home.

Our conversations were so God-focused and spiritual. I could see her desire and hunger to go deeper with Him. That's what drew me to her. The Lord seemed to be opening the door to a close friendship, so much so that I felt comfortable gently challenging her in a way that I hoped would spur her to grow closer to God.

ADIE:

One day Jeremy sat me down and said, "You're jaded." It was gutsy of him to say that, and I didn't like hearing those words, but the Lord totally used it because I had to admit that he was right. I had become distant from God, but at the same time I was

I STILL BELIEVE

hungry. I came back to Jeremy a few days later and thanked him for caring enough to notice and call me out on my spiritual condition. From that point on I was like, hmm, this guy is a mature believer. We started to bounce back and forth things the Lord was showing each of us. I wanted to know more about Jeremy's testimony. Having been in music, there was such a mutual understanding. We spoke much of the same language. My band was struggling a bit as well. There came a point where the music no longer became worth it. I didn't feel like we were in a good place spiritually. Meeting Jeremy and seeing how grounded he was, and hearing about Melissa's perspective, helped to awaken me. She is an amazing example of being sold out to the Lord. ....

Still, it was very clear that Adie wasn't my type, and I wasn't hers. I was this outgoing, jock-looking guy—"Hey, I work out!"—and she was this quiet, kind-of-shy rocker. But we became really good friends and had fun together. And man, I loved that she was so receptive to the things of the Lord, and clearly craving more of Jesus.

At some point as our friendship deepened, it hit me that I was feeling super-guilty about having such a good time with a girl other than Melissa. When that wave crashed down on me, I remember saying out loud, "Man, I can't do this." It had only been a year and eight months since I had said goodbye to my wife in that hospital room. After the realization dawned on me, I tried to push away from Adrienne, even though I was feeling more and more drawn to her every day.

Our relationship started growing, and it was obvious we were good friends. I did wonder if something more might come of it. We talked so easily. I could tell that he was pulling back. I said to a friend of mine, "I think he's gonna call this off."...

As I prayed about things, God spoke to my heart and said, "If I'm blessing you with something, don't question it too much. Receive my blessing." I also remembered the words that Melissa had spoken to me during her illness—words that must have been hard for her to say: "It's okay. If God brings somebody else, I want you to be happy..."

All these emotions poured out as Adrienne and I grew closer. I was overwhelmed. It was scary and exhilarating. One day as we were talking, it came to light that we were attracted to each other beyond just friendship. After that conversation, I bolted—not physically, but emotionally. Or at least I tried to run. I just wanted to go out and minister. I didn't need the distraction of a serious relationship. The timing couldn't be right, could it? I asked her if we could get some dinner one night. My intention was to tell her we needed to back off and stop the momentum of our relationship.

ADIE: ....

I could tell he was scared about things, you know, unsure about what should happen next. He pulled me aside and asked me to dinner. When we got to the restaurant and sat down, I had a feeling he was going to tell me we couldn't see each other anymore. But he threw me a curve ball. ....

Over dinner, I had planned to say something like, "We can't do this, it's not going to work, and we need to move on." But instead, I looked at her, and what came out of my mouth was, "Can you imagine spending the rest of your life with me? I mean, do you feel like you could marry me?"

What? Had I really just said that? She smiled even as she looked startled.

"Yes," she said.

"Okay," I replied, breathing out and laughing. "I've got to be honest. I came here tonight to kind of break it off with you. I've been feeling so much guilt and uncertainty. It's just overwhelming. But I couldn't. That's what came out. I've been through too much to play games, so...I hope you don't mind that I just asked you such a serious question."

"It's totally fine," she responded. "I'm glad we can just lay it all out like that."

ADIE: ....
We didn't eat much of our dinner. We just sat there kind of staring at each other thinking, *What just happened?* ....

Well, so much for slowing down the momentum of the relationship! Over the next few weeks and months, we became closer and closer. It seemed that a bright new chapter of life was dawning. I was so grateful to the Lord's healing work in my heart, and now, here was an unexpected gift in the midst of it all. This didn't mean the road ahead would be an easy one, but we looked forward to walking it out with Him.

CHAPTER 13

Breathe the Breath of Life

By December of 2002, things had moved so quickly with Adrienne that I wanted to take her home to see my parents, my sister and my brothers in Indiana. The first time I had told them about her, they had been shocked. She and I were so completely different from each other and, of course, this was the first time I had been talking about anyone else since Melissa. But when Adrienne finally came up to Indiana in January of 2003, my family was warm and welcoming to her. It didn't take long for her grace and sweetness to win them over.

During our visit, she went to the grocery store with my mom, who shared at great length about all we had gone through with Melissa, and what she had meant to me and to our family. My mom later said she appreciated Adie's compassion. "By the end of our talk, we were both crying," my mom recalled.

When I was alone with my mom and dad during the visit, I turned things up a notch, telling them, "She really is the one for me." Honestly, they were not thrilled about that at first, especially my mom and my sister. It wasn't easy for them to face this significant step in letting go of Melissa. But again, as they got to know Adie, any hint of resistance melted away. In fact, the Lord used her in many ways to help them through their own grieving. They had loved Melissa and, naturally, considered her a member of our family. Adie didn't come in and try to intrude on their sadness or replace Melissa. On the contrary, she was so gentle, patient and caring as she talked and listened.

Really, she was like a breath of fresh air that God breathed into our circumstances. My family felt the same level of comfort with her that I had when we first began talking on the Festival Con Dios tour.

At this time, a wedding photo of Melissa and me still hung in my family's living room. My mom admitted that she was having a hard time taking it down. Looking at the photo one afternoon, she said to Adie, "I don't know why it is so hard for me to take that down right now. But I want you to know the day you and Jeremy get married, it will be gone." Adie understood completely and responded with her usual graciousness.

ADIE: ....

Those first few months after our dinner on the tour were amazing...and also intense. I was coming out of a really dry place spiritually. When it came to dealing with Melissa, God gave us such an incredible grace. We never struggled with it. We were friends, so we talked about everything. Every once in a while I would say to Jeremy, "I'm feeling insecure today." And we would talk about it. But he would never compare me to her. I never felt that. He didn't put any expectation on me to live up to.

I'm really glad to have shared that season with him, as a friend, to walk through the healing process alongside him. It was never my heart to come in and 'take over.' There were times when Jeremy would wonder if he should stop sharing his testimony about Melissa, and I would speak into that: "God has used her to touch my heart, and so many other hearts, and that's part of who you are; don't think for a minute that I am going to get in the way of this. I know how it ministers to people. I've seen the impact. This is too important."...

In April of 2003, I formally asked Adrienne to marry me. We had already talked about marriage at the restaurant during our "break-up" dinner, so I was fairly confident that she would say "Yes" to my proposal. (Thank goodness, she did.) We set the date for December of that year.

She continued to blossom in the Lord during our engagement. She was pressing in and discovering new depths of God's presence, soaking in the Word, hearing His voice. It was *awesome* to watch. In fact, at one point I felt like saying, "Slow down! You're growing ahead of me!"

About a month before the wedding, she went with my mom to California to attend a retreat for pastors' wives. There, for the first time, she met Melissa's sisters, Megan and Heather, who were also attending.

ADIE: ....—...

They were both so sweet. It wasn't awkward at all. We hit it off immediately, and we kept in touch after the retreat. It wasn't until later that I met Melissa's

I STILL BELIEVE

parents, and that Jeremy saw them again for the first time. I did send them a wedding invitation, and on the anniversary of Melissa's passing, we send them flowers or a note to let them know we're praying for them and thinking of them. I want to be respectful of all they've been through. ....

At that same retreat, Adie spent some time talking with Tammy Courson, the second wife of Jon Courson, the pastor who had helped lead me to the Lord and had welcomed Ryan and me to his home in Oregon not long after Melissa's passing. Having walked through his own trial, he had ministered to me with such love and graciousness. Now, it was Tammy's turn to speak into my fiancée's life.

ADIE: ....
God really used that conversation. Being in the same state of mind, Tammy was able to speak godly truth and encourage me how to walk through things with Jeremy and have the right heart. She said, "There are certain places not to go in your mind, not comparing yourself." Jeremy never did, but as a girl I have to have self-control in my mind. It's fruitless, going down some of those roads. She gave examples of how she walked out different scenarios with Jon.

She challenged me, "If Jeremy never shared about you from the stage, and only shared about Melissa, would you be okay with that?" ....

"Yes," I said, "because I see the power of what God has done through her life, and the strength of Jeremy's testimony of walking by faith."

That was a good check in my heart, to remember that it's not about me, or even about Melissa, but it's about the work of the Lord in people's lives, and that God is faithful.

If I didn't have the Lord, I would not have been secure enough to support Jeremy in what he was doing. Along the way, I've met some insecure second wives. The things they've said to me are heartbreaking—things like, "I know what you're going through, honey. You can't ever live up to that, so don't even try." I don't feel that way, and thank God I never have. ....

It also helped Adrienne that my family embraced her and made it clear how much they valued her as my future wife. My dad pulled her aside one day and said, "I just want you to know that we love Melissa, but she's with Jesus now and you're here, and we do see you as a part of the family." Adie told me how much that meant to her. As my dad recalled later, "We were looking through pictures of Melissa and Jeremy one day when Adie was around. I could just tell she needed to hear that. I gave her a big hug. I also told her, 'God has selected you to be a tool to help heal my son. You're part of the healing plan for Jeremy.'"

ADIE: ....
In all of it, I tried to put myself in his family's shoes.

If that was me, and I had just gone through that, how would I feel? I didn't expect them to be over Melissa's passing within a certain timeframe. There were many times when Jeremy and I would cry together, talk it through, and know that another little piece of the healing was taking place. ....

Melissa's sister Heather had shared a powerful testimony with Adrienne: The passing of her sister, Heather said, was a tragedy that God used in her life to draw her closer to Himself. In her grieving, she had found comfort in the Lord as she never had before. Now, her spiritual walk was deeper and richer than ever. That was an amazing encouragement to Adie—and to me.

ADIE: ....

Melissa's perspective on life, cancer and God had such a domino effect on everyone around her. Had her heart been bitter, it would have severed ties with everybody along the way. Her heart for the Lord is incredible. As a result of that, her sister could stand up and testify about God's goodness even in the face of her sister's passing. It shows you how a positive and godly attitude can accomplish so much good. When the time is right, I will gladly tell our children all about Melissa. ....

CHAPTER 14

Glowing

On December 15, 2003, when I was 25 and Adie was 22, we exchanged our vows in a small ceremony attended by family and friends in my hometown of Lafayette, Indiana. As I stood at the front of the church awaiting my bride, my heart pounded and my mind swirled with thoughts. It was slightly surreal, but I was mostly overwhelmed with gratitude and anticipation.

My mom later said, "The thing I remember most...Adie had her wedding gown on. She was radiant! While living with us during the engagement, she had changed from a shy, sweet girl into a confident, Godly woman. I had truly seen the transformation before my eyes, but on the wedding day it struck me. The love of her earthly and heavenly bridegroom had turned her into a beautiful bride! She glowed with Jesus."

I stood at the front beside my dad, who had gladly accepted our invitation to perform the ceremony. When Adrienne walked into my line of sight in the back of the church,

I couldn't help but start crying tears of joy and thankfulness. My mom's assessment was right on target: Adie was glowing. I knew she was the perfect woman for me, God's gift, a sign of redemptive hope.

I looked over at my dad, who was also crying. Later on he said, "Yes, I wept through that one, too. I thought, *Oh my goodness, pull yourself together here. You've got to speak to the congregation in just a minute.* They were tears of joy, tears of happiness."

The song "Here I Am To Worship" played as Adie processed down the aisle. Before exchanging our vows, we entered into a time of worship led by my good friend Jean-Luc. It was unreal! The presence of the Lord filled the room. That is *exactly* what we wanted. We were there to honor God and bow down before Him, because He is our king, and we wanted to set the tone for the rest of our lives with His glory firmly on display.

His Kingship was easier to picture because of a creative spark that the Lord gave to Adrienne. As she had prayed about our wedding day, God had spoken to her heart the theme of *crowns.* She had hand-made all of our invitations and included small, wire crowns on each one. And she had made several crowns to adorn the church to help everyone there focus on the fact that God is not only our Lord and our Savior, but also our King. (She still loves crowns and loves to meditate on the royalty of God.)

ADIE: ....

The Lord gave me Isaiah 35:10, which says, "And the ransomed of the Lord will return. They will enter Zion with singing; everlasting joy will crown their heads. Gladness and joy will overtake them, and sorrow and sighing will flee away." That scripture was prophetic for us. When we became engaged, Jeremy's sister had said she felt the Lord was going to lead us out in joy. I always loved crowns anyway, so I thought, *How cool is that?* ....

We had written our own vows to exchange. It was hard for me to think about saying the phrase "'til death do us part" or "as long as we both shall live," so we kind of wrote around that part. At the end of the ceremony, we kissed and walked down the aisle together, feeling thrilled that our journey as husband and wife had begun.

In the weeks and months following our wedding, the doors of God's ministry through my music began to open even wider. I started work on a third record, *Restored*, and began doing more and larger concerts. It was a powerful time, made all the sweeter because I was entering it with a new bride and a deep sense of hope for what might lie ahead.

CHAPTER 15

Joyous Arrivals

*I*n early 2004, just two months into our marriage, Adie and I received some big news. Happy news. WHOA news. Yes... *that* kind of news: We were expecting a baby.

When we learned of the pregnancy, all we could do was laugh, hug each other and say, "Wow, Lord! Look what You are doing already." Some might wonder if it was a bit too early in our marriage to think about expanding the family, but we truly felt ready and open to whatever God had for us in His perfect timing.

ADIE:

Jeremy had wanted to have kids. It was his heart's desire. I love kids as well, and I definitely wanted to be a mom. Being so young and in the band, I felt like I had experienced a whole lot. So from the get-go, we knew we wanted kids. Our marriage started on such a different level, because we had to talk about so much before we got married. We talked and talked about really deep life stuff. I didn't feel like we needed much time just to get to know each other. ....

Our first child, Isabella Rose (Bella), was born on September 25, 2004. A year-and-a-half later, on April 5, 2006, we welcomed Arianne Mae (Arie). The girls are the most *amazing* blessings anyone could imagine. I love being a daddy, and I love seeing these precious ones discover the world around them. If all of us could view what God has created through the wondrous eyes of children, we would be much better off. Jesus certainly had a little something to say about that concept: "I tell you the truth, unless you change and become like little children, you will never enter the kingdom of heaven." [35]

Perfect Love's Cast

Parenting isn't all easy stuff, of course...and I'm not just talking about runny noses, temper tantrums or the chicken-nugget smell that's impossible to get out of the backseat. On a deeper level, I have waged a battle with fear when it comes to my children. It's interesting to me that I haven't felt any fear of losing Adrienne. I'm not sure why, but that's not anything I've had to confront. However, the story is much different with our girls. When each of them was born, I found myself feeling a weight of anxiety as I wondered, *Would God possibly think of taking one of them home?* I felt so much fatherly love for them that the idea of having to let them go petrified me. These thoughts and emotions would become so pervasive that I would hold my daughters extra close and pray extra hard for their protection. I'm not saying it was rational, but the fear was real.

....

[35] *Matthew 18:3*

During the years since our first child was born, the Lord has been delivering me from these fears, but I am still learning to trust Him in this area. At one point, when I was alone crying out to Him about my fears and about how much I love the girls, God spoke a gentle but firm word to my heart: "Do you not understand how much I love *you*, Jeremy? I love you perfectly, so much more than you could ever love your children." It was not quite the message I expected to hear from Him. I thought He might remind me of how much He loves *the girls*. But of course He could see all the way down to the root of my struggle, and so He spoke words that would meet me there.

I spent a little bit of time processing what He was saying. The Lord's character and essence *is* love,[36] the Word tells us that He is love. It also tells us that He loves us beyond what we could ever fathom. It hit me that if I could really understand His love and how He feels about me—how generously He wants to pour into my life, both in the present age and in the age to come—then I could get free from these fears that were besetting me. In other words, the more we embrace the depth of our Heavenly Father's everlasting care and concern for us, the easier it is to believe that all is well. No matter what happens on this side of heaven, we can be certain that He holds it all in His hands and knows the end from the beginning.

"Just trust Me," the Lord was reminding me. "Trust Me. Trust Me. Trust Me." As I prayed that day, God took me to a time-tested promise: "There is no fear in love. But perfect love casts out fear, because fear has to do with punishment. The

---

[36] *1 John 4:16*

one who fears is not made perfect in love."[37] The verse was a balm to my spirit. I repeated the words over and over.

I am still just beginning to grasp the truth that His love is the only perfect kind. As I "get" that to a greater degree, not only does it comfort me and wash away my fears, but it leads me to love God more and want to honor Him more fully in all that I think, say and do.

Afraid to Hurt

In the course of wrestling with fear, I realized I was afraid of the pain and heartache that I had experienced through Melissa's passing. It might sound selfish, but I feared ever feeling that way again. I realized that no matter what happened, all would be fine in the end, because I had dealt with some of the worst pain you could go through. But I was scared to walk through the pain again, because, well, the pain *hurts*. That was more my fear, and that's what God dealt with me on. He brought me to a place where I could proclaim, "Lord, I believe that You will walk with me through whatever pain I will have to face in the future. By Your grace, I will not be afraid of the pain."

What I have walked through has refined me. It hasn't defined me—this is not who I am, "the guy whose wife passed away and who has a powerful testimony because of that"— but it *has* refined me and deepened my dependence on the Rock of my salvation.

A friend whose son went home to be with the Lord told me, "Before this happened, I thought I had a strong relationship with God, but I was only in the meadow near the Cross.

---

[37] 1 John 4:18

I STILL BELIEVE

After it happened, I went to the foot of the Cross and stayed there." Suffering can refine us like nothing else can, if we see it as a temporary, necessary part of how we "grow up" into Christ.

As the Scriptures remind us, "In this you greatly rejoice, though now for a little while you may have had to suffer grief in all kinds of trials."[38] We find even more insight on this subject from Paul:

> *"Therefore we do not lose heart. Even though our outward man is perishing, yet the inward man is being renewed day by day. For our light affliction, which is but for a moment, is working for us a far more exceeding and eternal weight of glory, while we do not look at the things which are seen, but at the things which are not seen. For the things which are seen are temporary, but the things which are not seen are eternal."[39]*

[38] *1 Peter 1:6*
[39] *2 Corinthians 4:16-18*

CHAPTER 16

Back on My Feet Again

I continued to write songs from the heart, and many of the messages God gave me resonated with more and more listeners. Stories from people touched by the music and by my testimony kept pouring in. During the two years after our wedding, the success we experienced included Dove awards, widespread radio play, headlining tours and rising sales. The Gospel Music Association honored me with its New Artist of the Year award in 2004, along with Male Vocalist of the Year in 2004 and 2005, and Recorded Song of the Year in 2005 for "Stay."

With all of this attention came the expansion of what we were doing—more touring, more people involved in the process, more logistics to manage and think about. As anyone who has been part of Christian music can attest—or really, part of any form of large ministry/outreach/church—it can easily become consuming. It's possible to lose the proper focus even with the very best of intentions. Being around ministry for much of my life, I was aware of the traps and trappings that Satan can use to derail us from the pure pursuit of the Great Commission.[40]

During this season, I was still seeking God, still looking to honor Him...and yet, as the months went by, something seemed to be missing. Adrienne and I were doing great: more deeply in love, excited about our growing family. But the pace of our lives was relentless, and I was spending many hours on the details of this ministry that God had birthed.

Redirected

One day in 2005, a pastor friend whom I trusted pulled me aside and asked, "Jeremy, who's steering this ship? Is it the Lord, or is it you?"

His words pierced me, and the look of loving concern on his face cut right to the core. I had been feeling uneasy about things anyway, and God really used that question to make me pause and reevaluate. Honestly, I knew that *I* had been steering the ship—trying to guide the way as everything became bigger and better, working night and day in a vain attempt to control the outcomes. Yes, it's good to ask questions—What's next, Lord? Where do You want this ministry to go?—and to aim for excellence in all that we do, working with all of our heart as for the Lord and not for men.[41] But we have to wait for the Lord's leading and confirmation before moving ahead. That's the hard part! The uneasiness I felt was a sign that I had gotten out in front of God's guidance and was in need of a course correction. It wasn't like I was doing anything deliberately disobedient or

---

40 *Matthew 28:18-20*
41 *Colossians 3:23*

blatantly immoral in the eyes of the Lord. It was a matter of relinquishing control back to Him.

My dad also served as a voice of influence during this time. He liked to say, "We can get so busy doing the work of the Lord that we forget the Lord of the work." I felt that battle and struggled to find balance. On the one hand, I wanted to keep the momentum going! I was out there serving the Lord. *God is in this*, I kept thinking. He was, and He was using my music and testimony to bring large doses of encouragement and blessings to many people. But it was tempting to get caught up in all of the busyness and become distracted.

The true heartbeat of Jesus can fade out of our hearing if we let too much other noise into the mix. In my heart, I was taking control. It was a *false* sense of control—a total illusion. And yet it was easy to slip into the place of saying, "I'm doing this, I'm working hard, I'm succeeding, I'm ministering to people." (Yeah...there are *way* too many "I"s in that self-centered mindset.)

Pretty soon, "I" was seriously burned out. The Lord had propelled me into music ministry so purely, with gratitude, joy and humility. Now, I still felt grateful, but, honestly, my prayer had deteriorated into thinking more along the lines of, "Thanks, God...but I've got it from here." I'm ashamed to admit that, but it was true. What's more, my joy had waned. The enemy who comes to "steal, kill and destroy"[42] seemed to have found a way to rob me of any sense of contentment. I felt overwhelmed. My cry would often be, "Why am I not at peace, Lord? Where is the joy?"

---

[42] John 10:10a

I STILL BELIEVE

More Than Earthly Treasure

A combination of the Holy Spirit's conviction and the voices of wise men speaking into my life got my attention. I needed to get into the Word, so I carved out some time to refocus on the Scriptures. After some dedicated times of prayer, a lot of searching and talking with leaders and friends, I reawakened to a deeper sense of the Lord's presence.

One day in particular, I remember doing a media interview, sharing my testimony and Melissa's story. I recounted the time when she had said, "If one person were to accept Jesus Christ because of this..." Right then, it hit me again how much the Lord had done—all of the people who had come to Jesus or gone deeper with Him as a result of what we experienced.

After the interview, I sat down and just started weeping. That was a good thing—the dam was breaking. I prayed, "Lord, I want my focus to stay on You. I want You to be my first love again. I want to be led by You into the next season. You are in control, not me!"

He broke me down in a good way, and that day I wrote the song "Beyond Measure" as an expression of my desire to submit to the leading and Lordship of Jesus in all aspects of my life—as a man, a husband, a father and an artist.

(Verse 1)
The fog has finally cleared to see,
The beautiful life You've given me
To feel the breeze of my newborn's gentle breath
With one to walk hand in hand,

To share this life that You have planned
It's like a storybook with dreams that are meant to see
Every next step is an extraordinary scene

(Chorus)
I know that I've been given more than beyond measure
I come alive when I see beyond my fears
I know that I've been given more than earthly treasure
I come alive when I've broken down and given You control

(Verse 2)
I've faced a great tragedy,
But have seen the works of what You bring
A display of faith that You give
I don't know if I will ever understand
The depth of what it is You've done inside
But I know that I won't find
any worth apart from You

Everything that I have
Has been given so unselfishly
And shown that even when I don't deserve
You always show the fullness of Your love

The line, "I come alive when I've broken down and given You control," summed up where I was. I needed a transfusion of *real* life—the kind that could only spring from relinquishing my illusion of control.

The song also represented a renewed appreciation for God's good gifts. "I know that I've been given more than beyond measure..." It was true: I had been blessed immensely. I had the freedom to travel far and wide, sing songs, lead worship, watch the Lord touch lives through this ministry, come home to a beautiful wife and an awesome little daughter (this was before Arie came along), and see my family's needs met. For me, it was never about making tons of money or achieving a huge amount of notoriety, even though God started to provide some of those added blessings.

The peripheral things had become too important, and now I was realizing afresh: *All that matters is God.* He wants our hearts. The Bible is clear on that point in a number of places. For example, "Jesus answered, 'Love the Lord your God with all your heart and with all your soul and with all your strength and with all your mind...'"[43] And "...seek first His kingdom and His righteousness, and all these things will be given to you as well."[44]

God was all I had growing up in Indiana when my family fell to our knees praying for groceries. He was all I had at the private Christian high school when I scrubbed toilets after school to cover my tuition. He was all I had in California, when I lived with my friend's Grandma Marge and bummed rides from friends. He was all I had in the darkest moments after Melissa had gone home. And He wanted to continue to be my all, even as I experienced the kind of "success" that can lead us to shift our trust elsewhere.

Can you relate to what I'm saying? I'm almost positive that you can, at some level. It's no secret that our world is

[43] *Luke 10:27*
[44] *Matthew 6:33*

full of distractions. So many voices clamor for our attention: *This is the next thing. You must get this. You have to buy that. This will make you happy.* The key for me during this time of drifting off course was to get away from the noise whenever I could, dig into the Word, and listen for the still, small voice of the Holy Spirit speaking.

When I finally tuned in enough to hear it, the Lord gently but firmly reminded me: "I want you to love Me and rest in My love for you. I'll take care of everything else. I'm in control anyway, not you. Your illusion of power is just that, and it needs to be broken down."

Thanks be to God, He showed Himself faithful to perform the breaking in a way that didn't crush me but built me up for the next chapters of my life and ministry.

Grief with Hope

One of the chapters that awaited Adrienne and me was far from the pleasant kind. In August of 2009, as we had just entered the second trimester with our third child, we wrote the following blog and posted it to share with our friends and fans. The message is voiced from Adie's point of view:

Hi everyone. We have sad news to share with you. As some of you may know from my tweet, it was our baby check-up yesterday. I went in and they could not find the baby's heartbeat. This could be normal at my stage, but they sent me to have an ultrasound, from which we learned that our precious little one's heart had stopped a week earlier. The baby has gone to be with Jesus. It was a hard day for us yesterday, but praise the Lord Jeremy was home and he has been such a rock for me. God has overwhelmed us with His love and peace. We know He is faithful and don't doubt for a minute that He is in control. We are so thankful for the hope we have in Christ. We had an amazing time reading scripture together this morning and just sharing what God has done and all that He is doing in our lives. We know we are very blessed to have our two sweet little girls. Please pray that our eyes will continue to stay on Him. Also for my body to heal quickly...

We went on to quote from the tender, heartfelt cry found in Psalm 16:

"Preserve me, O God, for in You I put my trust. O my soul, you have said to the Lord, 'You are my Lord, my goodness is nothing apart from You.' O Lord, You are the portion of my inheritance and my cup; You maintain my lot. The lines have fallen to me in pleasant places; yes, I have a good inheritance. I will bless the Lord who has given me counsel; my heart also instructs me in the night seasons. I have set the Lord always before me; because He is at my right hand I shall not be moved. Therefore my heart is glad, and my glory rejoices; my flesh also will rest in hope. For You will not leave my soul in Sheol, nor will You allow Your Holy One to see corruption. You will show me the path of life; in Your presence is fullness of joy; at Your right hand are pleasures forevermore."

This was a difficult time for us. We grieved the loss of the life that we believed was being "knit together" fearfully and wonderfully. [45] We know that we're bound to experience hard times on this side of heaven, but that doesn't make them any easier to endure. Even so, we knew that our only real response was to cling to the belief that this was somehow

---

[45] Psalm 139

part of God's higher, better plan—a plan that won't become clear until we meet Jesus face to face.

Psalm 16 provided immense comfort to us. It is such a rich example of crying out in desperation while at the same time proclaiming the goodness and faithfulness of God. In fact, if you are walking through any kind of sad or challenging time right now, I would encourage you to back up and read the words of the psalm again. Read them slowly, let them sink in, and ask the Lord to help you believe them way down in the depths of your spirit. Let the words of the Scriptures draw you closer to Jesus, and hold on to Him for dear life.

As Adrienne reflected on this painful trial in our lives, she came away with some thoughts that I believe can speak hope to others dealing with similar circumstances.

ADIE: ....
Having our baby go to heaven gave me more perspective on what Jeremy struggled with as he had to let go of Melissa. As a mom, carrying a child and having a miscarriage during pregnancy is so personal, because it happens to your body. Just as no one who hasn't been pregnant can know what that is like, no one who hasn't had this happen to them can know what the pain feels like. It becomes almost like your own, solitary trial. It was similar with Jeremy and Melissa. If you haven't walked through a trial of that magnitude, it's hard to truly relate to the pain and sadness he was feeling. So, I felt as if I could relate to his pain more now in some ways. It hurts so much, but you hold on to your trust in God.

It's hard, but there is such a sweetness of the presence of the Lord in sadness that is definitely supernatural. We comfort others in the way that we've been comforted. I see the eternal worth and value of those hard life lessons, and the character that God has grown within us. The Lord has expanded our perspective and helped our hearts to get set on eternity, for us to realize this isn't our home. The question "Why?" will never be fully answered here. God requires us to walk by faith until that day. ....

CHAPTER 17

Speaking Louder than Before

Over the past several years, through joys and sorrows, I have seen God's hand continue to move in ways that are far beyond what my heart could have dreamed. Living through these times has made me want to climb to the top of the highest mountain—or at least to the top of my roof—and shout out for all to hear how awesome, mighty, faithful, loving, forgiving, healing, transforming and praiseworthy is the Lord our God. My desire has increased to do whatever is necessary *to let all the world know that Jesus saves.*

Along the way, my Heavenly Father has taught me that the fruit of the Spirit—love, joy, peace, patience, kindness, gentleness, goodness, faithfulness and self-control[46]—is really just a byproduct of spending time with the Lord. It results from dwelling in His Word and listening for His voice. As much as we might try, we can't go out and manufacture peace. We can't conjure joy or whip up faithfulness in the

---

[46] *Galatians 5:22-23*

microwave. Those things come to us only as we receive God's love, focus on bringing Him glory, stick close to Him, and live out the greatest commandment: loving God with everything we have and loving others in His name.

Psalm 24 asks two excellent questions and then answers them right away. First, the questions: "Who may ascend the hill of the Lord?" and "Who may stand in His holy place?" Now, the answers: "He who has clean hands and a pure heart, who does not lift up his soul to an idol or swear by what is false. He will receive blessing from the Lord and vindication from God his Savior. Such is the generation of those who seek Him, who seek Your face, O God of Jacob."[47]

What does it mean to be pure, and how do we do that? One thing I know for sure is that we have to get rid of those things in our lives that have become idols—even the "good" things, if they are more important than the Lord. Even a loving relationship, even our children, even our heart for sharing Jesus with others can become idols. Even in a marriage, God has to be first. If I were to focus more on Adrienne than I did on the Lord (and if she did the same with me), we would get in big trouble fast. We're going for the triangle effect: each of us walking with the Lord, looking up to Him, and growing closer to each other as a result.

My desire is to be the best husband and father I can be. I know I won't get there by striving for it in my own strength, or even by focusing on that end with laser-like intensity. No, the best way for me to see that desire become a reality is by seeking God first, seeking to walk in purity before Him, fleeing from idols and temptations, and crying out for His grace

---

[47] Psalm 24:3-6

and mercy to provide the strength I need to love my wife and children well.

What I'm after is that purity of heart that Jesus unfolded to His followers in the Sermon on the Mount: "Blessed are the pure in heart, for they shall see God."[48]

Precious Promises

The Bible contains a number of promises based on the equation, "If you do X, then the fruit will be Y." For example, "You will seek me and find me when you seek me with all your heart."[49] In other words, *if* we seek Him wholeheartedly, *then* we will find Him. The inverse is true as well: If we're *not* seeking the Lord with all of our heart, then we're *not* likely to find Him in the way that He intends for us to experience Him. To be clear, this doesn't mean He loves us any less or any more depending on what we do. Nothing, nothing, nothing can separate us from His love.[50] Still, if we lift our souls to other things, giving in to the chaos of distractions screaming for our attention, as a consequence we will miss out on the purity of heart required to "see God" the way He wants us to see Him.

In our era of social media, innovative mobile devices and lightning-fast wireless service, we might feel as if the world is more connected than ever before. I can flip open my laptop and be video-chatting with a friend across the globe in a matter of seconds. Music fans can debate back and forth about the latest downloads. Songs can be written, recorded and edited simultaneously by people scattered across continents. Adie

---

[48] *Matthew 5:8*
[49] *Jeremiah 29:13*
[50] *Romans 8:38-39*

and I can exchange photos of the kids while talking between our home near Nashville and tonight's concert destination. All of this is *very* useful, by the way. Technology is a great gift that I appreciate and use every day.

Still, I have to wonder: As connected as we are, what has happened to the *heart* connections between us and God and between us and each other? Have we become unintentionally superficial in our friendships? Could it be that we're actually more *disconnected* than we think? Maybe we need to wipe the slate clean and get back to loving Jesus and loving people as priority one. Rather than asking God to bless what we're doing, maybe we should set our hearts toward getting in on what He's already blessing.

As the Lord has deepened my heart, I have begun leading worship more as part of my concerts. The whole "show" is all about Him anyway, so it makes sense to point the people gathered there to a deeper experience of glorifying Him with our whole hearts. After the release of *Speaking Louder Than Before* in 2008, I began work on the music that would become *We Cry Out: The Worship Project*, an album released in August of 2010. The record is another expression of my growing desire to see God lifted higher and higher by a grateful people who realize just how worthy He is of our most extravagant praise.

Today, I can honestly say that I feel closer to the Lord than ever before. It's definitely a process, though, and by no means would I say I've "arrived" anywhere yet. God is still at work clearing away chaff from my life. My prayer, more times than I can count, is "Search me, O God, and see if there be any wicked way in me."[51] The more I've

---

[51] *Psalm 139*

prayed this, the more I've seen Him bringing junk to light that I didn't even know was there. I've sensed Him saying, "Look at what is still in your heart, Jeremy. I want you to let it go."

Many times, I have found that letting go is an essential part of finding the freedom we crave. Sometimes when we're crying out, "God, help me!" His answer might be, "I want to help you, but you've got to let go first." It's up to us to let go of control, to let go of a misplaced desire, to let go of a person we have put on a pedestal—whatever it is, we need to lay it down at the feet of Jesus in order to create space in our lives for Him to come in and bring healing.

Boiling It Down

The bottom line for me is this: As I seek to walk with Jesus and look back—over six months, two years, five years—is there unmistakable evidence of growth? He doesn't expect perfection, but He wants to see a willing heart that is growing closer to His own heart. (If we have any doubt about this truth, we need only look to King David. He made a huge mess of things, and there were severe consequences for his sin, but God looked on his repentant heart, forgave him, and used him in mighty ways.)

The truth is that God doesn't *need* me at all; He could accomplish His desires in other ways through other people. But He *wants* me to be part of the mix. He says, "My son, are you willing or not? If you are, then let's go!"

In case anyone is wondering, I don't see myself as any more spiritual than you or anyone else. As believers, all of us are called to love Jesus and tell others about Him in our places of influence. A singer on a stage is no more or less important than a teacher, a police officer, a corporate executive or a stay-at-home mom.

One of the challenges we face in our culture is that even followers of Jesus have drifted away from a basic literacy of God's Word. At best, we tend to ignore the Scriptures and look first to other books (or movies or music) for inspiration and wisdom, rather than soaking ourselves in the Bible like "a tree planted by streams of water, which yields its fruit in season..."[52] If our generation would see the Lord's hand move in a mighty way in our land, we must get back to the building blocks of personal prayer, Bible study, fasting, exuberant worship and other spiritual disciplines. We are called to "spur one another on toward love and good deeds",[53] whatever that looks like where we live, work and play.

These are some of the things that I believe our generation needs to get back to— beginning with myself! If ever we start to lose hope that it's possible to influence our society and see revival spring up, we need only look back to the Scriptures themselves for example after example. (Remember one of my mom's favorite chapters, Hebrews 11?) I like to think about Josiah, who was only eight years old when he became king.[54] Despite taking over for his corrupt father Amon at such a young age, Josiah brought the people back to the word of the Lord, and the word of the Lord back to the people. He banished false gods and restored honor to the Most High. If Josiah could do it, certainly there are those in our day who can rise up and speak the truth in love.

....

[52] Psalm 1
[53] Hebrews 10:24
[54] See 2 Kings, chapters 21-23

Who Will Speak?

The question is: *Who?* Who will stand and say, not just with words but with actions, "It's time to get back to the Lord, get rid of these idols, and bathe ourselves in His Word"? Believe me, the Bible is as relevant today as it has ever been. We need to hide the Word of God fully in our hearts. We're all in this together. We are His workmanship (His *poeima*), "created in Christ Jesus to do good works, which God prepared in advance for us to do."[55] The great news is that He already sees a beautiful result from those works, since He's the one who came up with them in the first place.

As believers, we are being sanctified. He is setting us apart, cleansing us, seeing us as members of His "chosen people, a royal priesthood, a holy nation, a people belonging to God, that you may declare the praises of Him who called you out of darkness into His wonderful light."[56] He wants us to be a generation that is set apart, not just meshing with society.

Do we need to be able to relate to our culture? Of course we do. Jesus ate with tax collectors and hung out with sinners. But He didn't compromise who He was in the process. Our challenge is to be "in the world" but not to become corrupted by it.

As for me and for my house, that is our heart: to love Jesus more each day and to share of His faithfulness wherever we go. I can't love anyone unselfishly if I'm not spending time with God and in the Scriptures. That can only happen through and by the Holy Spirit at work in my life. When we spend time with the Lord and let Him speak into our lives,

---

[55] *Ephesians 2:10*
[56] *1 Peter 2:9*

I STILL BELIEVE

we can't help but then go out and love our neighbor as ourselves. And all of us living this out would make the world such a different place.

Higher Plan

People sometimes ask me, "Are you planning to be in music your whole life?" I'm not sure what the Lord has in store for my future, but I can say for certain that music is not my life. Christ is my life. I love writing, singing and playing songs that He gives me to share, but whatever He has for me in five or ten years, I want to be willing to step into it. I never want to hold so tightly to my vocation that I lose out on His higher plan. My aim is to hold tightly to my Savior while keeping a loose grip on the world and this temporal life, remembering the words of Jesus: "For where your treasure is, there your heart will be also."[57]

I try to live each day with this timeless truth in mind: "However, I consider my life worth nothing to me, if only I may finish the race and complete the task the Lord Jesus has given me—the task of testifying to the gospel of God's grace."[58] Truly, my life is not my own; it belongs to Jesus. I want to finish it someday, at His appointed time, and have Him say, "Well done, good and faithful servant."[59] The only way for me or anyone else to hear those words is to draw near to God and stay as close to Him as we can get, remaining accountable both to Him and to trusted friends who can help us stay on track.

---

[57] *Matthew 6:21 and Luke 12:34*
[58] *Acts 20:24*
[59] *Matthew 25:23*

If we do this, our generous Heavenly Father will give us exactly what we need to "speak louder than before" into the lives of the hurting, the hungry, and all who are desperate for much more fulfillment than this passing-away world can ever hope to provide.

CHAPTER 18

Hold on to what's being Held out

I have seen the many faces of fear
I have watched the tears fall plenty
from heartache and stress
So if life's journey has you weary and afraid
There's rest in the shadow of His wings...
—from "Healing Hand of God"

Late one night in 2009, as the tour bus drove us back toward Tennessee after a show in New York, I found myself praying about Melissa. Eight years after her passing, I had been thinking about all that we had walked through and wondering whether the story still had a place in the path of ministry that God had called me to travel.

Lord, do you want me to keep sharing this testimony? I prayed. *Should it have a part in the words that I speak publicly?* I had sensed the freedom to talk about the journey of walking with Melissa through cancer, feeling the pain of letting her go, watching as she surrendered her earthly life and went home into the arms of Jesus. But I had begun to think that chapter of my life had run its course, and that it might be time to leave it behind.

As I prayed into the night, I sensed the Lord laying on my heart story after story of people who had been touched in some way over the years by this testimony. Many of the thousands of e-mails, letters, comments and one-on-one encounters came to my mind—people struggling through deep valleys of loss or illness who had received a timely nugget of encouragement from a song, or a scripture, or a thought that the Lord had given me to speak from the stage, in video clips and interviews.

Time and time again, I have talked to people and heard variations of the same response: "Thank you so much for sharing how God brought you through this trial and showed His faithfulness. It gives me hope for what *I'm* facing."

As the bus rolled on, God reminded me that this painful trial is still a chapter of my life, and of Melissa's life, that has a purpose. I know that we've all moved on. I have been blessed with an amazing wife and two beautiful children. Adie and my girls are the most precious gifts imaginable, and I am so thankful for them. But what Melissa and I lived through together can still speak encouragement and hope to others.

The Lord led me to a great passage about trouble and comfort:

> "Blessed be the God and Father of our Lord Jesus Christ, the Father of mercies and God of all comfort, who comforts us in all our tribulation, that we may be able to comfort those who are in any trouble, with the

I STILL BELIEVE

*comfort with which we ourselves are comforted by God.
For as the sufferings of Christ abound in us, so our consolation also abounds through Christ. Now if we are
afflicted, it is for your consolation and salvation, which
is effective for enduring the same sufferings which we
also suffer. Or if we are comforted, it is for your consolation and salvation. And our hope for you is steadfast,
because we know that as you are partakers of the sufferings, so also you will partake of the consolation."* [60]

The bottom line of that passage for me is that if I have
gone through trouble and received God's comfort—and I
have—then it is my responsibility to extend that same comfort to others who are walking through similar troubles.

It is remarkable to me how faithful God has been, not
only to walk beside me through that painful season, but then
to heal my heart in the aftermath. He has long since restored
me from a deep, dark place back to a place of light and hope.
I never want to stop sharing about His faithfulness in my life.

My heart truly beats with a desire to share the truth of
God's Word with anyone who is hurting. I want to be a con-
duit that He uses to remind you of the astounding depth of
His care for you. "Cast all your cares upon Him, because He
cares for you." [61] I want to proclaim that the Lord is very near
to anyone who is going through pain and brokenness: "The
sacrifices of God are a broken spirit; a broken and contrite
heart, O God, You will not despise." [62]

---

[60] *2 Corinthians 1:3-7*
[61] *1 Peter 5:7*
[62] *Psalm 51:17*

You're Right Here

Whatever trial or tribulation we might be facing, God really is near. As one of my songs proclaims, we can know that He is "right here," not far away, ready to reach out and steady us when we're too weak to stand and wondering whether we have the strength for the next breath.

When it feels like we can't hold on to anything else, we can cling desperately to what's being held out to us: the "Healing Hand of God." As the chorus of that song puts it,

> *I have seen the healing hand of God*
> *Reaching out and mending broken hearts*
> *Taste and see the fullness of his peace*
> *And hold on to what's being held out*
> *The healing hand of God*

The Word of God never promises that we won't go through trials. Actually, it's pretty much a sure thing that we *will* go through them. In fact, James exhorts us to "consider it pure joy, my brethren, whenever you face trials of many kinds."[63] We aren't guaranteed a perfect life. We're going to struggle and endure hardships. And yet God *does* promise that in our trials, He will stand right next to us and be there every moment. He will be faithful to lead us and guide us, to breathe life into us and heal our hearts.

You might be reading this and thinking that you haven't experienced a life-and-death trial, or a particularly painful

---

[63] *James 1:2*

I STILL BELIEVE

circumstance. How, then, can you relate to someone who has, or is, walking through that? I would encourage you, first, to pray for compassion for those who are enduring trials. Pray for understanding. God will give you an understanding and a compassion that is from Him, because His words proclaim the truth. He knows what suffering is like. He can relate, because He has endured it. And because His spirit lives within each of His followers, He *can* and *will* do amazing work in your heart as you open it to Him. He will give you words of encouragement to share with the hurting, and He will direct your steps in how to walk alongside them with tenderness, comfort and hope.

Melissa said it best on that day when I saw her radiating the peace of her Savior in the hospital bed: "if just one person accepted Jesus...it would all be worth it."

Those words continue to inspire me, especially when I consider that many lives, not just one, have been drawn closer to Jesus—or drawn to Jesus for the first time—through the story of her courageous faith.

She clung to the healing hand of God, trusted Him completely, and walked through the valley of the shadow into the embrace of the Savior who was welcoming her home.

Home. Home to a place of no more suffering, no more sickness, no more pain.

All of us who remain on this side for a little while longer must find our truest purpose in holding tightly to His hand, while at the same time reaching out to the lost, the lonely and the burdened.

In His name, we offer comfort. We extend mercy. We hold out the same great, glorious hope of Christ that has taken hold of us.

Through our lives and through our love, we invite the world to "taste and see the fullness of His peace"—a peace beyond measure that we have discovered in the healing hand of God.

EPILOGUE

There will be a Day

My dad recently reflected on all that transpired after Melissa's passing and in the years since that painful day in 2001. I like the way he put it:

"We were in a fog, and it was hard to see out of it. It seemed like it might last forever. But then, all of a sudden, it happened so fast that the Lord began to change things. He brought Adrienne into Jeremy's life, they were married, the music ministry really took off—it felt almost miraculous. God was saying to us, 'I allowed this for a reason. The Gospel is going to go out stronger, and many, many people will be ministered to because of this story.' To think of where we are now is surreal. The fog has lifted, and the way ahead seems clearer now."

As clear as things are now compared to the way I felt during Melissa's illness and after her passing, I still see only partially, imperfectly, incompletely. I have tasted and seen the goodness of the Lord in the form of life after life changed because of the testimony of God's faithfulness, even in the midst of pain and sadness. I have seen the Lord redeem pain and "work for the good"[64] out of what began as the sad passing of a beloved young woman.

There will be a day, however, when everything truly becomes crystal clear. Answers to the mysteries that leave us scratching our heads (and aching deep in our souls) will be revealed. Pain will give way to ultimate healing, strife to unbreakable peace, and sadness to unending joy. It's going to be a great day! It's the day that Jean-Luc was talking about after Melissa's memorial service when he said to me, "My friend, this is why we need to hasten the day...Jesus is coming back."

On that day, we will walk into the waiting arms of our Savior, look into His eyes, and know Him fully, as we were created to know Him from the beginning.

We will see Melissa, even more beautiful than she was during her earthly life, worshipping our Lord without sickness or pain.

We will see the little baby that Adie and I released into Heaven's arms in 2009.

We will see all of the fellow believers we have ever loved who have gone on to be with the Lord.

And I will see my precious brother Josh freed from the limitations of Down syndrome, able to experience the fullness of understanding and an even deeper joy of life in the presence of our Lord.

I can hardly wait...but while I do wait, I'll wait in the knowledge that Jesus promises not only life everlasting, but also a life of inner contentment and peace now, despite the

---

[64] Romans 8:28

painful circumstances that we must inevitably encounter while living in this broken world.

May the words of this song that He gave me become an anthem of truth and triumph for all of us:

"THERE WILL BE A DAY"

(Verse 1)
I try to hold on to this world with everything I have
But I feel the weight of what it brings,
and the hurt that tries to grab
The many trials that seem to never end,
His Word declares this truth,
that we will enter in this rest with wonders anew

(Chorus)
But I hold on to this hope and the promise that He
brings
That there will be a place with no more suffering
There will be a day with no more tears, no more pain,
and no more fears
There will be a day when the burdens of this place, will
be no more
We'll see Jesus face to face
But until that day, we'll hold on to You always

(Verse 2)
I know the journey seems so long,
you feel you're walking on your own

But there has never been a step
that you've walked out all alone
Troubled soul don't lose your heart
'cause joy and peace He brings
And the beauty that's in store
outweighs the hurt of life's sting

(Bridge)
I can't wait until that day
When the very one I've lived for always
Will wipe away the sorrow that I've faced
To touch the scars that rescued me
From a life of shame and misery
This is why, this is why I sing....

(Chorus)
There will be a day with no more tears,
no more pain, and no more fears
There will be a day when the burdens of this place,
will be no more, we'll see Jesus face to face
There will be a day,
He'll wipe away the tears,
He'll wipe away the tears,
He'll wipe away the tears
There will be a day...

About the Authors

Jeremy Camp allows a transparent view of his life and daily walk with Christ to be an encouragement and a testimony of God's faithfulness. His thoughtful, honest lyrics and booming voice have earned him multitudes of fans worldwide, more than 3 million records sold, 5 GMA Dove Awards, 20 number-one radio hits, 1 Grammy nomination, 2 American Music Award nominations, 3 ASCAP Songwriter of the Year awards, and 2 Male Vocalist of the Year honors. He would be the first to tell you that he is very thankful for the recognition and humbled that God would use him in this way. First and foremost, Jeremy is a man of God seeking Him in the ups and downs of life and asking for his life to be a light. His joys are his Savior, his amazing wife, his children, and his family and friends. Jeremy's prayer is that God would use his life and the words of this book to draw you closer to Him.

For more information about Jeremy please visit:
jeremycamp.com

Jeremy was assisted in the research, writing and editing of this book by **Phil Newman**, an author and communications specialist who lives with his family in Franklin, Tennessee.

Contact:
phil@newmanifest.com

Jeremy & Melissa

Melissa & a friend

Jeremy & Melissa (wearing white) in worship

Mission trip in Hawaii
(praying on the beach)

Jeremy &
friend Jean-Luc

(from the Kry)

Jeremy playing with the Kry

Melissa's bridal shower

from left to right:
her sister Heather,
Melissa,
& sister Megan

Oct 21st, 2000

Jeremy & Pastor Joey

Jeremy & Adrienne

(Festival Con Dios 2002
when they met)

December 15th, 2003

Tom & Teri Camp

Isabella 09-25-04

Arie & Bella

Bella, Adrienne,
Arie, Jeremy